PT Sports Questions

Get an Edge Over the Competition

Pass the SCS Exam Without Breaking the Bank

100 Multiple Choice Questions

Sports physical therapy specific questions

Acute Injury and Management Decision Making

Dr. Matthew P. Brancaleone, DPT, PT, AT, CSCS
Board Certified Specialist in Sports Physical Therapy

First Author: Matthew P. Brancaleone
Content Editor: Cody J. Mansfield
Copyright Editor: Aaron S. Mansfield
Graphic Designer: Eric Hostetter
Illustrator: Samantha Williams

Dedication

This book is dedicated to my wife Ashley and my son Vincent for your unwavering love, support, and encouragement.

PREFACE

Congratulations on your pursuit to becoming a specialist in sports physical therapy. This book was designed to help physical therapists pass the sports certified specialty (SCS) examination.

This book is the second release from Fast Twitch Press. PT Sports Questions is a 100-question multiple-choice test. The questions were designed to be specific to sports physical therapy and include acute injury and management decision-making questions.

The test taker will view the question. Slide to the next page, and see if they answered accurately. There will be an explanation of the correct answer and a reference to an article that supports it. It is recommended that you read the articles associated with the questions that you have answered incorrectly.

Passing the SCS examination is a huge accomplishment. Your pursuit of this specialization is a testament to your passion for our profession and goal of delivering exemplary care to your patients.

Good luck and study hard.

Cody J. Mansfield, PT, DPT, OCS, AT
Physical Therapist
Board Certified Specialist in Orthopedic Physical Therapy
Fellow of the American Academy of Orthopaedic Manual Physical Therapists

About the Author:

Matt's clinical interests include working with athletes of all different ages on and off of the field with a variety of sport and orthopedic pathologies. He is actively involved in Ohio State's outreach program providing medical coverage for club and recreational sports as well as the marching band.

Matt has experience working with the deaf and hard-of-hearing population through previous work at Gallaudet University in Washington, D.C. and service as an athletic trainer for the USA Deaf Sports Federation and 2013 Deaflympic Games in Sofia, Bulgaria and the 2017 Deaflympic Summer Games in Samsun, Turkey.

Matt is involved with three research projects specific to deaf and hard-of-hearing athletes. He is currently investigating satisfaction levels at the Deaflympic Games, studying baseline ImPACT scores and baseline scores from the Clinical Test of Sensory Organization and Balance.

Outside the clinic and sports coverage, he enjoys spending time with his family, playing ice hockey and participating in endurance events.

Education

Bachelor of Arts, Athletic Training, Central Michigan University, 2010

Doctorate of Physical Therapy, Central Michigan University, 2014

Sports Physical Therapy residency, The Ohio State University, 2015

Check us out on social media:

Website: FastTwitchPress.com
Facebook: Facebook.com/fasttwitchpress
Twitter: @MansfieldCody
          @FastTwitchPress

Check out all our books:

1) What is the most important aspect of the pre-participation exam?

     a. History
     b. Medical examination
     c. Musculoskeletal examination
     d. Performance testing

1) What is the most important aspect of the pre-participation exam?

  a. History
    a. **A complete medical and family history should act as the cornerstone for the pre-participation exam. More than 90% of musculoskeletal injuries can be detected by taking a thorough history.**
  b. Medical examination
  c. Musculoskeletal examination
  d. Performance testing

Conley KM, Bolin DJ, Carek PJ, Konin JG, Neal TL, Violette D. National Athletic Trainers' Association position statement: preparticipation physical examinations and disqualifying conditions. *J Athl Train*. 2014;49(1):102-120.

2) Which of the following is not part of the meniscal composite examination to detect meniscal tears?

        a. McMurray's sign
        b. Thessaly test
        c. Patient history of mechanical symptoms
        d. Overpressure into knee extension

2) Which of the following is not part of the meniscal composite examination to detect meniscal tears?

   a. Positive McMurray's sign
   b. Positive Thessaly test
      a. The meniscal composite examination consists of (1) patient history of "catching" or "locking," (2) pain with forced hyperextension, (3) pain with maximum flexion, (4) positive McMurray's sign, and (5) knee joint line tenderness to palpation.
   c. Patient history of mechanical symptoms
   d. Pain with overpressure into knee extension

Lowery DJ, Farley T, Wing DW, Sterett WI, Steadman JR. A clinical composite score accurately detect meniscal pathology. *Arthroscopy*. 2006;22(11):1174-1179.

3) During the deceleration (follow through) phase of pitching, teres minor, infraspinatus, and the posterior deltoid muscle are responsible for what?

        a. Act concentrically as a restraint to humeral head translation
        b. Act eccentrically as a restraint to humeral head translation
        c. Act isometrically as a restraint to humeral head translation
        d. B and C only

3) During the deceleration (follow through) phase of pitching, teres minor, infraspinatus, and the posterior deltoid muscle are responsible for what?

    a. Act concentrically as a restraint to humeral head translation
    b. Act eccentrically as a restraint to humeral head translation
        a. Teres minor, infraspinatus, and the posterior deltoid act eccentrically to restraint the humeral head translation. Additionally, the serratus anterior and rhomboids help to stabilize the scapula during deceleration during follow through.
    c. Act isometrically as a restraint to humeral head translation
    d. B and C only

Calabrese G. Pitching mechanics, revisited. *Int J Sports Phys Ther.* 2013;8(5):652-660.

4) A high school softball player presents to you in the clinic. She states that she tried to pick up her teammate to celebrate after a walk-off homerun a month ago. She now presents to the clinic with scapular winging and weakness with shoulder forward flexion. What nerve is most likely involved?

a. Suprascapular nerve
b. Subscapular nerve
c. Long thoracic nerve
d. Axillary nerve

4) A high school softball player presents to you in the clinic. She states that she tried to pick up her teammate to celebrate after a walk-off homerun a month ago. She now presents to the clinic with scapular winging and weakness with shoulder forward flexion. What nerve is most likely involved?

    a. Suprascapular nerve
    b. Subscapular nerve
    c. Long thoracic nerve
        a. Trauma to the long thoracic nerve typically occurs from a hit to the shoulder or repetitive activities. Associated symptoms may include neck and shoulder pain that becomes worse with overhead activities. Scapular winging and shoulder flexion weakness may be apparent upon examination.
    d. Axillary nerve

Neal SL, Fields KB. Peripheral nerve entrapment and injury in the upper extremity. *Am Fam Phys*. 2010;81(2);147-155.

5) You are evaluating a patient status-post right anterior cruciate ligament reconstruction. You are screening the patient for possible deep vein thrombosis. Which of the following is not part of the Wells criteria?

      a. Calf swelling ≥ 3 cm compared to the asymptomatic calf
      b. Unilateral pitting edema
      c. Localized tenderness along the deep vein system
      d. Shortness of breath

5) You are evaluating a patient status-post right anterior cruciate ligament reconstruction. You are screening the patient for possible deep vein thrombosis. Which of the following is not part of the Wells criteria?

    a. Calf swelling ≥ 3 cm compared to the asymptomatic calf
    b. Unilateral pitting edema
    c. Localized tenderness along the deep vein system
    d. Shortness of breath
        a. The Wells criteria for deep venous thrombosis includes:
            i.   (+1) Active cancer✶
            ii. (+1) Paralysis or recent plaster immobilization of the lower extremities✶
            iii. (+1) Recently bedridden for 3 days or more, or major surgery within the previous 12 weeks requiring general or regional anesthesia
            iv. (+1) Localized tenderness along the distribution of the deep venous system
            v. (+1) Entire leg swollen
            vi. (+1) Pitting edema confined to the symptomatic leg
            vii. (+1) Collateral superficial veins (nonvaricose)
            viii. (+1) Previously documented deep vein thrombosis
            ix. (-2) Alternative diagnosis at least as likely as deep vein thrombosis
            A score of 2 or higher indicates the probability of a deep vein thrombosis is likely. A score less than two indicates that the probability of a deep vein thrombosis is unlikely.

Wells PS, Anderson DR, Rodger M, et al. Evaluation of D-dimer in the diagnosis of suspected deep-vein thrombosis. *N Engl J Med.* 2003;349:1227-1235.

6) You are evaluating an athlete in the clinic who presents with hip pain. He states that the pain started gradually over the last year. He reports pain located on the lateral hip in the shape of a "C" and states the pain is "deep." He also reports popping and clicking. Functionally, getting up from a deep squat position is uncomfortable. What is the most likely cause of the symptoms?

      a. Slipped capital femoral epiphysis
      b. Femoral stress fracture
      c. Snapping hip syndrome
      d. Femoral acetabular impingement

6) You are evaluating an athlete in the clinic who presents with hip pain. He states that the pain started gradually over the last year. He reports pain located on the lateral hip in the shape of a "C" and states the pain is "deep." He also reports popping and clicking. Functionally, getting up from a deep squat position is uncomfortable. What is the most likely cause of the symptoms?

      a. Slipped capital femoral epiphysis
      b. Femoral stress fracture
      c. Snapping hip syndrome
      d. Femoral acetabular impingement
          a. A patient suffering from femoral acetabular impingement will have a history of gradual or acute precipitating episode. Some will describe decreased flexibility on the involved side compared to teammates. Mechanical symptoms may be present described as sharp, stabbing pain or catching during lateral or twisting movements. Maximum flexion and resisted extension from a flexion position may be painful.

Thomas Byrd JW. Femoracetabular impingement in athletes, part 1: cause and assessment. *Sports Health*. 2010;2(4): 321-333.

7) You are performing an initial evaluation on a high school ballet dancer who reports of posterior ankle pain. She reports that it began gradually but now she has to modify her techniques for relevé. Additionally, she reports posterior ankle pain during push-off activities.. Clinical examination reveals tenderness located between Achilles tendon and the peroneal tendons during weight bearing and palpation. What is the most likely cause of the symptoms?

      a. Osteochondritis dissecans
      b. Achilles tendonitis
      c. Os trigonum syndrome
      d. Medial malleolus stress fracture.

7) You are performing an initial evaluation on a high school ballet dancer who reports of posterior ankle pain. She reports that it began gradually but now she has to modify her techniques for relevé. Additionally, she reports posterior ankle pain during push-off activities... Clinical examination reveals tenderness located between Achilles tendon and the peroneal tendons during weight bearing and palpation. What is the most likely cause of the symptoms?

- a. Osteochondritis dissecans
- b. Achilles tendonitis
- **c. Os trigonum syndrome**
    - **a. Os trignoum results from a bony and soft tissue compression in the posterior tibiocalcaneal interval. This condition is most occurs from repetitive plantar flexion stress and is primarily seen in ballet dancers and soccer players. Clinical findings will include decreased plantar flexion range of motion, decreased plantarflexion strength, tenderness between the Achilles tendon and the peroneal tendons during weight bearing and palpation, posterior ankle pain during push-off activities, and posterior ankle edema. This condition may also be seen with flexor hallicus longus tenosynovitis secondary to constant pressure on the os trignoum from the flexor hallicus longus tendon.**
- d. Medial malleolus stress fracture.

Nault ML, Kocher MS, Micheli LJ. Os trigonum syndrome. *J Am Acad Orthop Surg.* 2014; 22(9):545-553.

8) You are performing an initial evaluation on an adolescent girl who is complaining of foot pain. She reports pain located over the second metatarsal head that is worse with weight bearing activities. She reports that it also wakes her up from sleeping often. Upon examination, she shows swelling and crepitus over the second metatarsal phalangeal joint. She also demonstrates a positive Lachman's test of the metatarsal joint. What is the most likely cause of the symptoms?

      a. Freiberg's disease
      b. Kohler's disease
      c. Sinding-Larsen-Johansson disease
      d. Sever's disease

8) You are performing an initial evaluation on an adolescent girl who is complaining of foot pain. She reports pain located over the second metatarsal head that is worse with weight bearing activities. She reports that it also wakes her up from sleeping often. Upon examination, she shows swelling and crepitus over the second metatarsal phalangeal joint. She also demonstrates a positive Lachman's test of the metatarsal joint. What is the most likely cause of the symptoms?

> a. **Freiberg's disease**
>> a. **Freiberg's disease or Freiberg's infraction is avascular necrosis that occurs in the metatarsal. Most common it occurs in the second metatarsal of adolescent females. Clinical presentation typically includes swelling and hyperkeratosis beneath the affected metatarsal head. Crepitus and loose bodies may also be palpable. Hallux valgus deformity is found in about half of the cases. The clinical presentation of Freiberg's disease is similar to other conditions such as stress fractures, joint sepsis, metatarsalgia, etc. Therefore, other conditions should be ruled out via imaging and other diagnosis techniques.**
> b. Kohler's disease ؛ Navicular bone
> c. Sinding-Larsen-Johansson disease
> d. Sever's disease

Carmont MR, Rees RJ, Blundell CM. Current concepts review: Freiberg's disease. *Foot Ankle Int*. 2009;30(2):167-176.

9) You are evaluating a 13-year-old overweight male who is complaining of left groin pain. He reports just beginning basketball season a few weeks ago. He reports having an antalgic gait. During the physical examination, he has limited passive and active hip flexion, hip abduction, and hip internal rotation secondary to pain. What is the most likely cause of the symptoms?

      a. Slipped capital femoral epiphysis
      b. Legg-Calve-Perthes disease
      c. Snapping hip syndrome
      d. Hip labral tear

9) You are evaluating a 13-year-old overweight male who is complaining of left groin pain. He reports just beginning basketball season a few weeks ago. He reports having an antalgic gait. During the physical examination, he has limited passive and active hip flexion, hip abduction, and hip internal rotation secondary to pain. What is the most likely cause of the symptoms?

      a. Slipped capital femoral epiphysis
            a. Slipped capital femoral epiphysis occurs when the growth plate of the proximal femoral physis is weak which results in displacement from it's normal position. This condition is common in overweight males between the ages of 5 and 8. Clinical presentation will include an antalgic gait, pain in the hip, groin, thigh, or knee. The patient will have a positive leg roll, range of motion deficits in hip flexion, hip abduction, and hip internal rotation. Thigh or calf muscle atrophy may also be apparent.
      b. Legg-Calve-Perthes disease BS to head of femur
      c. Snapping hip syndrome   gets disrupted
      d. Hip labral tear

Peck D. Slipped capital femoral epiphysis: diagnosis and management. *Am Fam Phys*. 2010;82(3):258-262.

10) You are performing an initial evaluation on a high school football athlete who presents to the clinic with complaints of right thigh pain. He reports it started after getting hit with the crown of another athlete's helmet to his anterior thigh about 6 weeks ago. He says his coach told him it was a quadriceps strain and to ice it; however, it has not improved. He reports a "little lump" on the anterior aspect of his thigh and pain with running and attempts as physical activity. Today he presents with decreased active and passive knee flexion compared to his uninvolved leg, pain with resisted knee extension. What is the most likely cause of the symptoms?

      a. Grade II quadriceps strain
      b. Femoral stress fracture
      c. Myositis ossificans
      d. Ruptured quadriceps tendon

10) You are performing an initial evaluation on a high school football athlete who presents to the clinic with complaints of right thigh pain. He reports it started after getting hit with the crown of another athlete's helmet to his anterior thigh about 6 weeks ago. He says his coach told him it was a quadriceps strain and to ice it; however, it has not improved. He reports a "little lump" on the anterior aspect of his thigh and pain with running and attempts as physical activity. Today he presents with decreased active and passive knee flexion compared to his uninvolved leg, pain with resisted knee extension. What is the most likely cause of the symptoms?

> a. Grade II quadriceps strain
> b. Femoral stress fracture
> c. **Myositis ossificans**
> > a. **Myositis ossificans is characterized by calcifications in the muscle secondary to an injury to that muscle. Most commonly this occurs in the arms or the quadriceps. The bone will typically grow for 2-4 months following the trauma and will become mature bone after a few months. Clinical presentation will include decreased ability to flex knee, palpable lump in the involved muscle, and pain to the involved area during physical activity.**
> d. Ruptured quadriceps tendon

Beiner JM, Mokl P. Muscle contusion injury and myositis ossificans traumatica. *Clin Orthop Relat Res*. 2002;403:S110-S119.

11) You are performing an initial evaluation on a male who suffered a "skier's thumb" injury after falling on his hockey stick during a practice. During the physical exam, you note swelling at the 1st metacarpal phalangeal joint and a mass felt on the ulnar side of the metacarpal phalangeal joint. In addition to the skier's thumb, what should the clinician be concerned about?

      a. Stener lesion
      b. Metacarpal fracture
      c. Scaphoid fracture
      d. Triangular fibrocartilage complex injury

11) You are performing an initial evaluation male who suffered a skier's thumb injury after falling on his hockey stick during a practice. During the physical exam, you note swelling at the1st metacarpal phalangeal joint and a mass felt on the ulnar side of the metacarpal phalangeal joint. In addition to the skier's thumb, what should the clinician be concerned about?

   a. **Stener lesion**
      a. **A skier's thumb is a partial or complete rupture of the ulnar ligament of the 1st metacarpal phalangeal joint. A Stener lesion occurs when distal end of the ulnar collateral ligament and the aponeurosis of the adductor pollicis become intertwined at the base of the proximal phalanx. Since the UCL is no longer in contact with the insertional site, it does not have the ability to heal on it's own. Clinical presentation of a Stener lesion will include swelling at the 1st metacarpal phalangeal joint and a palpable mass in the same area.**
   b. 1st Metacarpal fracture
   c. Scaphoid fracture
   d. Triangular fibrocartilage complex injury

Mahajan M, Rhemrev SJ. Rupture of the ulnar collateral ligament of the thumb – a review. *Int J Emerg Med*. 2013;6(31).

12) You are performing an initial evaluation on a female soccer player. She reports she was practicing corner kicks during practice when she had immediate groin pain. She describes the pain as dull or aching at rest and sharp during running or kicking activities. Clinical presentation includes antalgic gait, abdominal pain, and decreased abductor and adductor muscle strength. What is the most likely cause of the symptoms?

      a. Inguinal hernia
      b. Femoral acetabular impingement
      c. Legg-Calve-Perthes disease
      d. Osteitis pubis

12) You are performing an initial evaluation on a female soccer player. She reports she was practicing corner kicks during practice when she had immediate groin pain. She describes the pain as dull or aching at rest and sharp during running or kicking activities. Clinical presentation includes antalgic gait, abdominal pain, and decreased abductor and adductor muscle strength. What is the most likely cause of the symptoms?

- a. Inguinal hernia
- b. Femoral acetabular impingement
- c. Legg-Calve-Perthes disease
- **d. Osteitis pubis**
    - **a. Osteitis pubis is an inflammatory pathology of the pubic symphysis. It is common in activities that include kicking, changing direction, and accelerations or decelerations. Individuals will present with pain over the public symphysis or medial groin pain, decreased muscular strength of hip adductors and abductors, and possibly antalgic gait. Individuals may also present with decreased internal or external rotation of the hip.**

Hitti CJ, Stevens KJ, Jamati MK, Garza D, Matheson GO. Athletic osteitis pubis. *Sports Med*. 2011;41(5):361-376.

13) You are performing an initial evaluation on a 12-year-old male pitcher who is complaining of medial elbow pain. He reports that it began mid-season but has progressively become worse throughout the remainder of the season. Clinical presentation includes swelling over the medial elbow, loss of full extension, and tenderness of the medial elbow. Radiographs are normal. What is the most likely diagnosis?

     a. Medial elbow apophysitis
     b. Ulnar collateral ligament injury
     c. Nursemaid's elbow
     d. Panner's disease

13) You are performing an initial evaluation on a 12-year-old male pitcher who is complaining of medial elbow pain. He reports that it began mid-season but has progressively become worse throughout the remainder of the season. Clinical presentation includes swelling over the medial elbow, loss of full extension, and tenderness of the medial elbow. Radiographs are normal. What is the most likely cause of the symptoms?

   a. Medial elbow apophysitis
      a. Medial elbow apophysitis or little leaguer's elbow is a common condition in throwing athletes between the ages of 9 and 12 years old. Medial elbow pain will be apparent during throwing activities. They also may have decreased throwing speed and accuracy. Clinical presentation will include elbow swelling, loss of motion, and medial elbow tenderness.
   b. Ulnar collateral ligament injury
   c. Nursemaid's elbow
   d. Panner's disease

Cassas KJ, Cassettari-Wayhs A. Childhood and adolescent sports-related overuse injuries. *Am Fam Phys*. 2006;73(6): 1014-1022.

14) You are performing an initial evaluation on a 17-year-old offensive lineman who is complaining of back pain. He reports back pain that was only apparent during activity but now has progressed to having pain at rest. Clinical presentation includes hyper-lordotic posture, limited lumbar range of motion, hamstring tightness, and a positive stork test. What is the most likely cause of the symptoms?

    a. Spondylolysis
    b. Vertebral disc pathology
    c. Scheuermann's disease
    d. Sacroiliac dysfunction

14) You are performing an initial evaluation on a 17-year-old offensive lineman who is complaining of back pain. He reports back pain that was only apparent during activity but now has progressed to having pain at rest. Clinical presentation includes hyper-lordotic posture, limited lumbar range of motion, hamstring tightness, and a positive stork test. What is the most likely cause of the symptoms?

    a. Spondylolysis

        a. **Spondylolysis is described as a pars interarticular defect. It commonly occurs in athletes that require repeated back hyperextension such as football linemen or gymnasts. Clinical examination may include hyper-lordotic curve, limited lumbar range of motion, hamstring tightness, tenderness over affected segment and a positive stork test.**

    b. Vertebral disc pathology

    c. Scheuermann's disease

    d. Sacroiliac dysfunction

Cassas KJ, Cassettari-Wayhs A. Childhood and adolescent sports-related overuse injuries. *Am Fam Phys*. 2006;73(6): 1014-1022.

15) You are performing a preseason screen on a professional baseball team. You are taking the external and internal rotation measurements of both the throwing and non-throwing arm. Your clinical findings for one of the pitchers include the total rotational motion at 90° of abduction on both the pitching and non-pitching arm. What is the minimum deficit of total rotational motion bilaterally that will put this athlete at risk for injury?

    a. 3°
    b. 5°
    c. 8°
    d. 10°

15) You are performing a preseason screen on a professional baseball team. You are taking the external and internal rotation measurements of both the throwing and non-throwing arm. Your clinical findings for one of the pitchers include the total rotational motion at 90° of abduction on both the pitching and non-pitching arm. What is the minimum deficit of total rotational motion bilaterally that will put this athlete at risk for injury?

    a. 3°
    b. 5°
        a. Total rotational motion is calculated by adding shoulder external and internal rotation at 90° of shoulder abduction. In professional pitchers, a difference of 5° bilaterally in total rotation motion puts those athletes at a higher risk for injury.
    c. 8°
    d. 10°

Wilk KE, Macrina LC, Arrigo C. Passive range of motion characteristics in the overhead baseball pitcher and their implications for rehabilitation. *Clin Orthop Relat Res*. 2012;470(6):1586-1594.

16) You are performing an initial examination on a collegiate pitcher in the clinic referred for a diagnosis of "thoracic outlet syndrome." The patient reports that symptoms occur following a strenuous pitching effort. These symptoms include arm swelling, cyanosis, and distended superficial veins over the upper arm, shoulder, and chest. What type of thoracic outlet syndrome is this athlete suffering from?

      a. Venous thoracic outlet syndrome
      b. Arterial thoracic outlet syndrome
      c. Neurogenic thoracic outlet syndrome
      d. Lymphatic thoracic outlet syndrome

16) You are performing an initial examination on a collegiate pitcher in the clinic referred for a diagnosis of "thoracic outlet syndrome." The patient reports that symptoms occur following a strenuous pitching effort. These symptoms include arm swelling, cyanosis, and distended superficial veins over the upper arm, shoulder, and chest. What type of thoracic outlet syndrome is this athlete suffering from?

    a. Venous thoracic outlet syndrome
        a. Venous thoracic outlet syndrome is characterized by arm swelling, cyanosis, and distended superficial veins over the upper arm, shoulder and chest that is preceded by activity with the arms.
    b. Arterial thoracic outlet syndrome
    c. Neurogenic thoracic outlet syndrome
    d. Lymphatic thoracic outlet syndrome

Sanders RJ, Hammond SL, Rao NM. Diagnosis of thoracic outlet syndrome. *J Vasc Surg*. 2007;46(3): 601-604.

17) Which of the following is not a part of the subacromial impingement clinical prediction rule?

      a. Hawkins-Kennedy test
      b. Painful arc sign
      c. Infraspinatus manual muscle test
      d. Neer's impingement

17) Which of the following is not a part of the subacromial impingement clinical prediction rule?

    a. Hawkins-Kennedy test
    b. Painful arc sign
    c. Infraspinatus manual muscle test
    d. Neer's impingement
        a. Neer's impingement is not a test associated with the subacromial impingement clinical prediction rule. Hawkins Kennedy test, painful arc sign and infraspinatus manual muscle test make up the subacromial impingement clinical prediction rule. If there are positive findings for the above, there is positive likelihood ratio of 10.6 and a post-test probability of 95% that the patient has subacromial impingement.

Park HB, et al. Diagnostic accuracy of clinical tests for the different degrees of subacromial impingement syndrome. *J Bone Joint Surg Am.* 2005; 87(7): 1446-1455.

18) Which of the following athletes would you expect to have Panner's disease?

      a. 24-year-old softball pitcher
      b. 9-year-old baseball pitcher
      c. 24-year-old basketball player
      d. 9-year-old soccer player

18) Which of the following athletes would you expect to have Panner's disease?

      a. 24-year-old softball pitcher
      b. 9-year-old baseball pitcher
            a. Panner's disease is the development of osteochondrosis of the capitellum of the elbow. This disease commonly occurs in children who are younger than 10 years of age. Individuals with Panner's disease report a history of pain with valgus stretch (i.e. pitching) and pain and stiffness that is relieved by rest.
      c. 24-year-old basketball player
      d. 9-year-old soccer player

Claessen FM, Louwerens JK, Doornberg JB, van Dijk CN, Eygendaal D, van den Bekerom MP. Panner's disease: literature review and treatment recommendations. *J Child Orthop*. 2015;9:9-17.

19) You are evaluating a patient 3 weeks status-post anterior cruciate ligament reconstruction. To measure knee joint effusion, you perform the stroke test. The result of the test is the effusion spontaneously returns to the medial side after upstroke with no down stroke necessary. What grade would you give this result?

     a. 1+
     b. 2+
     c. 3+
     d. 4+

19) You are evaluating a patient 3 weeks status-post anterior cruciate ligament reconstruction. To measure knee joint effusion, you perform the stroke test. The result of the test is the effusion spontaneously returns to the medial side after upstroke with no down stroke necessary. What grade would you give this result?

- a. 1+
- **b. 2+**
  - **a. The results of the test would be a 2+. The stroke test is grade as follows**
    - i.   **Zero – No wave produced on down stroke**
    - ii. **Trace – Small wave on medial side with down stroke**
    - iii. **1+ - Larger bulge on medial side with down stroke**
    - iv. **2+ - Effusion spontaneously returns to medial side after upstroke (no down stroke necessary)**
    - v.   **3+ - So much fluid that it is not possible to move the effusion out of the medial aspect of the knee**
- c. 3+
- d. 4+

Sturgill LP, Synder-Mackler L, Manal TJ, Axe MJ. Interrater reliability of a clinical scale to assess knee joint effusion. *JOSPT*. 2009;39(12):845-849.

20) What clinical test is used to detect the presence of osteochondritis dissecans of the knee?

      a. Wilson's sign
      b. Steinman test
      c. Ege's test
      d. Dial test

20) What clinical test is used to detect the presence of osteochondritis dissecans of the knee?

    a. Wilson's sign
        a. Wilson's test is used to detect the presence of osteochondritis dissecans of the knee. It is performed by flexing the patient's knee to 90° and then grasping the foot and bringing the tibia into internal rotation. Then, ask the patient to extend their leg. The test is positive if the patient reports pain at 30° from full extension and the pain is relieved with external rotation of the tibia.
    b. Steinman test
    c. Ege's test
    d. Dial test

Conrad JM, Stanitski DL. Osteochondritis dissecans: Wilson's sign revisited. *Am J Sports Med.* 2003;31(5):777-778.

21) A 16-year-old male hockey player gets hit in the open ice from an opponent. He hits the ice and losses consciousness for about 30 seconds. After regaining consciousness, he complains of a headache and is slightly dizzy. At this time, you complete a SCAT-3. His symptom score is 9 and he is diagnosed with a concussion. Ten minutes later, he reports he is symptom free. Which of the following recommendations is appropriate for returning this athlete to play?

   a. He should not be allowed to return to play and he should be immediately transferred to a medical facility for advanced imaging
   b. Not allowed to return to play and should have reassessment by a medical professional
   c. He should be allowed to return to play with serial reassessments between break in play
   d. He should be allowed to return to play as long as this is his first concussion

21) A 16-year-old male hockey player gets hit in the open ice from an opponent. He hits the ice and losses consciousness for about 30 seconds. After regaining consciousness, he complains of a headache and is slightly dizzy. At this time, you complete a SCAT-3. His symptom score is 9 and he is diagnosed with a concussion. Ten minutes later, he reports he is symptom free. Which of the following recommendations is appropriate for returning this athlete to play?

    a. He should not be allowed to return to play and he should be immediately transferred to a medical facility for advanced imaging

    b. Not allowed to return to play and should have reassessment by a medical professional
        a. If an athlete is diagnosed with a concussion, they are not allowed to return to play on the same day of injury.

    c. He should be allowed to return to play with serial reassessments between break in play

    d. He should be allowed to return to play as long as this is his first concussion

McCrory P, Meeuwisse WH, Aubry M, et al. Consensus statement on concussion in sport: the 4th International Conference on Concussion in Sport held in Zurich, November 2012. *Br J Sports Med.* 2013;47:250-258.

22) A male rugby player suffered a concussion during a match 2 days ago. Today he completed rehabilitation stage 2 of the graduated return to play protocol without any symptoms during or following exercise. How long does the athlete have to wait to progress to stage 3 of the graduated return-to-play protocol?

    a. 1 hour
    b. 6 hours
    c. 24 hours
    d. 48 hours

22) A male rugby player suffered a concussion during a match 2 days ago. Today he completed rehabilitation phase 2 of the graduated return to play protocol without any symptoms during or following exercise. How long does the athlete have to wait to progress to phase 3 of the graduated return-to-play protocol?

     a. 1 hour
     b. 6 hours
     c. 24 hours
          a. The return to play protocol following a concussive episode is a 6-phase graduated plan. This includes: (1) No Activity (2) Light aerobic exercise (3) Sport-specific exercise (4) Non-contact training drills (5) Full-contact practice (6) Return to play. The athlete must be asymptomatic at the current phase in order to progress to the next and there should be 24 hours between each phase.
     d. 48 hours

McCrory P, Meeuwisse WH, Aubry M, et al. Consensus statement on concussion in sport: the 4th International Conference on Concussion in Sport held in Zurich, November 2012. *Br J Sports Med*. 2013;47:250-258.

23) A fracture to what aspect(s) of the scaphoid has the highest incidence of avascular necrosis?

      a. Distal fracture
      b. Middle fracture
      c. Proximal fracture
      d. Oblique fracture

23) A fracture to what aspect(s) of the scaphoid has the highest incidence of avascular necrosis?

    a. Distal fracture
    b. Middle fracture
    c. **Proximal fracture**
        a. **A proximal fracture is prone to avascular necrosis secondary to the path of the artery that supplies the scaphoid. The volar arterial branch supplies mainly the distal portion of the bone whereas the proximal pole relies entirely on intramedullary blood flow.**
    d. Oblique fracture

Hackney LA, Dodds SD. Assessment of scaphoid fracture healing. *Curr Rev Musculoskelet Med*. 2011;4(1):16-22.

24) You have been working with a professional volleyball player following a SLAP labral repair. You are going to isometrically test the athlete's external rotation (ER) and internal rotation (IR) strength. What is the ideal ER/IR ratio in normal healthy shoulders?

    a. 33%
    b. 50%
    c. 66%
    d. 100%

24) You have been working with a professional volleyball player following a SLAP labral repair. You are going to isometrically test the athlete's external rotation (ER) and internal rotation (IR) strength. What is the ideal ER/IR ratio in normal healthy shoulders?

      a. 33%
      b. 50%
      c. 66%
            a. Dynamic stabilization of the shoulder joint is thought to be achieved with appropriate balance between agonist and antagonist muscle groups. It is suggested that the external-to-internal rotator muscle strength ratio should be 66%-75%.
      d. 100%

Wilk KE, Meister K, Andrews JR. Current concepts in the rehabilitation of the overhead throwing athlete. *Am J Sports Med*. 2002;30(1):136–151.

25) You are working with a high school pitcher following UCL reconstruction. You have begun the return to throwing program with no set backs thus far. During today's session he became sore during warm up and it continued through the first 15 throws. According to the soreness rules, what would you recommend to the athlete?

      a. Stop and take one day off and repeat most recent throwing program workout

      b. Stop and take two days off. Upon return to throwing, drop down one step

      c. Advance to the next step

      d. Stop and take 3 days off. Upon return to throwing program, repeat most recent throwing program.

25) You are working with a high school pitcher following UCL reconstruction. You have begun the return to throwing program with no set backs thus far. During today's session he became sore during warm up and it continued through the first 15 throws. According to the soreness rules, what would you recommend to the athlete?

   a. Stop and take one day off and repeat most recent throwing program workout
   b. Stop and take two days off. Upon return to throwing, drop down one step
      a. According to the soreness rules, due to the athlete having soreness during the warm-up and through the first 15 throws, they must refrain from continuing with the current phase, take 2 days off, and when returning to throwing, to drop down to the previous phase.
   c. Advance to the next step
   d. Stop and take 3 days off. Upon return to throwing program, repeat most recent throwing program.

Axe M, Hurd W, Snyder-Mackler L. Data-based interval throwing programs for baseball players. *Sports Health*. 2009;1(2):145-153.

26) You are a physical therapist working with a collegiate DI pitcher who is post-operative UCL reconstruction. He was cleared and has completed a return to throwing program with no setbacks. He now asks you to give him feedback on his pitching biomechanics during the stride (early cocking) phase. Which one of the following is a possible biomechanical deficit seen during this phase of pitching?

    a. Elbow height at or above the shoulder with an elbow flexion angle between 80°–100°
    b. Stride length of 85-100% pitchers height
    c. Stride foot contact directed towards home plate or slightly towards third base (Right handed pitcher)
    d. Stride foot contact directed towards first base (right handed pitcher)

26) You are a physical therapist working with a collegiate DI pitcher who is post-operative UCL reconstruction. He was cleared and has completed a return to throwing program with no setbacks. He now asks you to give him feedback on his pitching biomechanics during the stride (early cocking) phase. Which one of the following is a possible biomechanical deficit seen during this phase of pitching?

    a. Elbow height at or above the shoulder with an elbow flexion angle between 80°–100°
    b. Stride length of 85-100% pitchers height
    c. Stride foot contact directed towards home plate or slightly towards third base (Right handed pitcher)
    d. **Stride foot contact directed towards first base (right handed pitcher)**
        a. **The stride foot contact directed towards first base as a right-handed pitcher is considered an open foot contact position. This can reduce ball velocity due to premature pelvic rotation.**

Calabrese GJ. Pitching mechanics, revisited. *IJSPT*. 2013;8(5):652-660.

27) You are treating a collegiate baseball athlete who is recovering from an ulnar collateral ligament reconstruction. The athlete had just begun rehabilitation following the docking procedure and is curious on when he will be able to begin the interval-throwing program. What is an appropriate response?

      a. 3 months post-operatively
      b. 4 months post-operatively
      c. 5 months post-operatively
      d. 6 months post-operatively

27) You are treating a collegiate baseball athlete who is recovering from an ulnar collateral ligament reconstruction. The athlete had just begun rehabilitation following the docking procedure and is curious on when he will be able to begin the interval-throwing program. What is an appropriate response?

        a. 3 months post-operatively
        b. 4 months post-operatively
            a. Following an ulnar collateral ligament reconstruction via docking procedure, an overhead throwing athlete would be expected to start an interval throwing program at 4 months. They would then progress to mound throwing and return to competition between 9 and 12 months post-operatively.
        c. 5 months post-operatively
        d. 6 months post-operatively

Ellenbecker TS, Wilk KE, Altchek DW, Andrews JR. Current concepts in rehabilitation following ulnar collateral ligament reconstruction. *Sports Health*. 2009;1(4):301-313.

28) You are treating a recreational runner who complains of patellofemoral pain. She is looking to reduce ground reaction forces through her knees and hips while running. What change in her running biomechanics could you suggest to achieve this goal?

     a. Increase stride length
     b. Increase trunk flexion
     c. Increase hip extension
     d. Increase cadence

28) You are treating a recreational runner who complains of patellofemoral pain. She is looking to reduce ground reaction forces through her knees and hips while running. What change in her running biomechanics could you suggest to achieve this goal?

    a. Increase stride length
    b. Increase trunk flexion
    c. Increase hip extension
    d. Increase cadence
        a. Compared to a preferred running speed, energy absorption is substantially decreased when cadence is increased by 10%.

Heiderscheit BC, Chumanov ES, Michalski MP, Wille CM, Ryan MB. Effects of step rate manipulation on joint mechanics during running. *Med Sci Sports Exerc.* 2012;43(2):296-302.

29) Following anterior cruciate ligament reconstruction, what percentage of athletes suffer a second ACL injury, either ipsilateral or contralateral, within 2 years of returning to sport?

      a. 10%
      b. 20%
      c. 30%
      d. 40%

29) Following anterior cruciate ligament reconstruction, what percentage of athletes suffer a second ACL injury, either ipsilateral or contralateral, within 2 years of returning to sport?

      a. 10%
      b. 20%
      c. 30%
            a. Within 2 years of returning to sport following ACL reconstruction, 30% of individuals will suffer a second ACL injury. Of the 30%, 21% occurred on the contralateral limb and 9% occurred on the ipsilateral limb.
      d. 40%

Paterno MV, Rauh MJ, Schmitt LC, Ford KR, Hewett TE. Incidence of second ACL injuries 2 years afte primary ACL reconstruction and return to sport. *Am J Sports Med*. 2014;42(7):1567-1573.

30) You are working the sidelines at a collegiate rugby game. An athlete approaches you who is unable actively extend his 4th distal interphalangeal joint (DIP). No fracture is present following imaging. Which is not appropriate management for this condition?

    a. Instruction not to flex DIP joint
    b. DIP joint splinted in neutral or slight hyperextension for 6 weeks
    c. Athletic participation is not allowed during splinting period
    d. If skin blanches, allow 10-20 minutes of "breathing" time between splint changes to decrease likelihood of maceration.

30) You are working the sidelines at a collegiate rugby game. An athlete approaches you who is unable actively extend his 4th distal interphalangeal joint (DIP). No fracture is present following imaging. Which is not appropriate management for this condition?

   a. Instruction not to flex DIP joint
   b. DIP joint splinted in neutral or slight hyperextension for 6 weeks
   c. **Athletic participation is not allowed during splinting period**
        a. **Athletic participation is allowed during the splinting period of a mallet finger injury; however, the DIP joint must stay splinted at all times including athletic participation.**
   d. If skin blanches, allow 10-20 minutes of "breathing" time between splint changes to decrease likelihood of maceration.

Leggit JC, Meko CJ. Acute finger injuries: Part I. tendons and ligaments. *Am Fam Phys*. 2006;73(5): 810-816.

31) You are performing a treatment session with a lacrosse athlete following meniscal repair. During today's treatment session, your focus is improving gait utilizing the therapeutic pool. In order facilitate 60-75% reduction in weight bearing, how high should the water level be?

      a. Chest deep water
      b. Abdominal deep water
      c. Thigh deep water
      d. Calf deep water

31) You are performing a treatment session with a lacrosse athlete following meniscal repair. During today's treatment session, your focus is improving gait utilizing the therapeutic pool. In order facilitate 60-75% reduction in weight bearing, how high should the water level be?

    a. Chest deep water
        a. Ambulating in chest deep water will result in 60-75% reduction in weight bearing. Normalizing ambulating following surgery will facilitate improvements in range of motion and appropriate muscular firing during dynamic activities.
    b. Abdominal deep water
    c. Thigh deep water
    d. Calf deep water

Cavanaugh JT, Killian SE. Rehabilitation following meniscal repair. *Curr Rev Muscoloskelet Med.* 2012;5(1):46-58.

32) You are in the final stages rehabilitating a high school female sprinter following a grade I hamstring strain. What should the focus on this final phase of rehabilitation be?

      a. Isometric hamstring strengthening
      b. Eccentric hamstring strengthening in a neutral state
      c. Concentric hamstring strengthening in a lengthened state
      d. Eccentric hamstring strengthening in a lengthened state

32) You are in the final stages rehabilitating a high school female sprinter following a grade I hamstring strain. What should the focus on this final phase of rehabilitation be?

    a. Isometric hamstring strengthening
    b. Eccentric hamstring strengthening in a neutral state
    c. Concentric hamstring strengthening in a lengthened state
    d. Eccentric hamstring strengthening in a lengthened state
        a. During the final phase of rehabilitating a hamstring strain, the focus should be hamstring strengthening in a lengthened state. This is secondary to most hamstring injuries occurring during an eccentric contraction while the hamstring is in a lengthened state (i.e. terminal swing phase of the sprinting cycle).

Schmitt B, Tim T, McHugh M. Hamstring injury rehabilitation and prevention of reinjury using lengthened state eccentric training: a new concept. *Inj J Sports Phys Ther.* 2012;7(3):333-341.

33) You are in the latter phase of anterior cruciate ligament reconstruction rehabilitation for a high school basketball player. You decide to perform a tuck jump assessment to examine her neuromuscular control. Which of the following is not a part of the assessment?

       a. Knee and thigh motion
       b. Foot position during landing
       c. Trunk position during landing
       d. Plyometric technique

33) You are in the latter phase of anterior cruciate ligament reconstruction rehabilitation for a high school basketball player. You decide to perform a tuck jump assessment to examine her neuromuscular control. Which of the following is not a part of the assessment?

> a. Knee and thigh motion
> b. Foot position during landing
> **c. Trunk position during landing**
>> **a. The tuck jump assessment is a high level plyometric activity that allows the clinician to assess neuromuscular deficits. The assessment consists of analyzing and scoring knee and thigh motion, foot position during landing, and plyometric technique.**
> d. Plyometric technique

Myer GD, Ford KR, Hewett TE. Tuck jump assessment for reducing anterior cruciate ligament injury risk. *Athl Ther Today*. 2008;13(5):39-44.

34) During a one-arm push up exercise at the later stage of rehabilitation following labral repair, which of the following muscles has the largest activation?

     a. Infraspinatus
     b. Anterior deltoid
     c. Posterior deltoid
     d. Pectoralis major

34) During a one-arm push up exercise at the later stage of rehabilitation following labral repair, which of the following muscles has the largest activation?

- **a. Infraspinatus**
    - **a. During a one-arm push-up, the infraspinatus was found to have the largest percent of maximum voluntary isometric contraction (MVIC) at 86%. Anterior deltoid measured at 46% MVIC, posterior deltoid measured at 74% MVIC, and pectoralis major at 44% MVIC.**
- b. Anterior deltoid
- c. Posterior deltoid
- d. Pectoralis major

Uhl TL, Carver TJ, Mattacola CG, Mair SD, Nitz AJ. Shoulder musculature activation during upper extremity weight-bearing exercise. *JOSPT*. 2003;33(3):109-117.

35) A meniscal tear in what zone has the least likelihood to generate a healing response?

      a. Red zone
      b. Red-white zone
      c. Grey zone
      d. White zone

35) A meniscal tear in what zone has the least likelihood to generate a healing response?

      a. Red-red zone
      b. Red-white zone
      c. Grey zone
      d. White-white zone
           a. The white-white zone is described as the inner two-thirds of the meniscus. This area of the meniscus is avascular. Due to the avascularity of this zone, it is the least likely to generate a healing response.

Mordecai SC, Al-Hadithy N, Ware HE, Gupte CM. Treatment of meniscal tears: an evidence based approach. *World J Orthop*. 2014;5(3):233-241.

36) Individuals who undergo an allograft anterior cruciate ligament reconstruction are how many times greater to suffer graft failure compared to those with an autograft reconstruction?

        a. 2 times
        b. 3 times
        c. 4 times
        d. 5 times

36) Individuals who undergo an allograft anterior cruciate ligament reconstruction are how many times greater to suffer graft failure compared to those with an autograft reconstruction?

    a. 2 times
    b. 3 times
    c. 4 times
        a. Individuals who have an allograft anterior cruciate ligament reconstruction were found to be 4 times at greater risk of graft failure compared to those with an autograft reconstruction. There was also a 2.3 times increase in allograft rupture for every 10-year decrease in age compared to autograft reconstruction.
    d. 5 times

Kaeding CC, Aros B, Pedroza A, Pifel E, et al. Allograft versus autograft anterior cruciate ligament reconstruction: predictors of failure from a MOON prospective longitudinal cohort. *Sports Health*. 2011;3(1):73-81.

37) You are adjusting a bike for a road cyclist who is complaining of anterior knee pain. You are concerned with the amount of knee flexion at the bottom of the down stroke. What is the appropriate amount of knee flexion at the bottom of the down stroke?

a. 0° to 5°
b. 10° to 15°
c. 20° to 25°
d. 30° to 35°

37) You are adjusting a bike for a road cyclist who is complaining of anterior knee pain You are concerned with the amount of knee flexion at the bottom of the down stroke. What is the appropriate amount of knee flexion at the bottom of the down stroke?

       a. 0° to 5°
       b. 10° to 15°
       c. 20° to 25°
           a. At the bottom of the down stroke, the knee flexion angle should measure between 20° and 25°. This angle can be adjusted by either raising or lowering the saddle height.
       d. 30° to 35°

Silberman MR, Webner D, Collina S, Shiple BJ. Road bicycle fit. *Clin J Sports Med*. 2005;15:271-276.

38) Subscapularis precautions are followed after shoulder surgery that involves the release and repair of the subscapularis tendon. Which of the following is not apart of the subscapularis precautions?

      a. No passive external rotation beyond 30°at 45° of abduction
      b. No external rotation "stretching"
      c. No active resistive internal rotation
      d. No passive internal rotation

38) Subscapularis precautions are followed after shoulder surgery that involves the release and repair of the subscapularis tendon. Which of the following is not apart of the subscapularis precautions?

  a. No passive external rotation beyond 30°at 45° of abduction
  b. No external rotation "stretching."
  c. No active resistive internal rotation
  d. No passive internal rotation
      a. Subscapularis precautions are typically followed for 6 weeks post-operatively. These precautions consist of no passive external rotation beyond 30°at 45° of abduction, no external rotation "stretching," and no active resisted internal rotation.

Ellenbecker TS, Bailie DS, Lamprecht D. Humeral resurfacing hemiarthroplasty with meniscal allograft in a young patient with glenohumeral osteoarthritis. *J Orthop Sports Phys Ther*. 2008;38(5):277-286.

39) You are treating a recreational runner with a diagnosis of right patellar tendinopathy. The patient reports 5/10 pain with running activities and navigating stairs. What type of tendon loading would be the most appropriate at this time?

     a. Isometric loading
     b. Isotonic (concentric) loading
     c. Isotonic (eccentric) loading
     d. Energy-storage loading

39) You are treating a recreational runner with a diagnosis of right patellar tendinopathy. The patient reports 5/10 pain with running activities and descending stairs. What type of tendon loading would be the most appropriate at this time?

      a. Isometric loading
          a. Isometric loading is the most appropriate at this stage of rehabilitation due to more than minimal pain occurring during isotonic activities such as navigating stairs. Five repetitions of 45 seconds, 2-3 times per day at 70% maximal voluntary contraction is recommended during this stage of rehabilitation.
      b. Isotonic (concentric) loading
      c. Isotonic (eccentric) loading
      d. Energy-storage loading

Malliaras P, Cook J, Purdam C, Rio E. Patellar tendinopathy: clinical diagnosis, load management, and advice for challenging case presentations. *J Orthop Sports Phys Ther*. 2015;45(11):887-898.

40) What is the suggested percentage of maximum voluntary isometric contraction needed in order to make strength gains?

       a. 40% to 50%
       b. 50% to 60%
       c. 60% to 70%
       d. 70% to 80%

40) What is the suggested minimum percentage of maximum voluntary isometric contraction needed in order to make strength gains?

> a. 40% to 50%
> **b. 50% to 60%**
>> **a. Muscle activation greater than 50% to 60% maximum voluntary isometric contraction has been suggested to make muscular strength gains.**
> c. 60% to 70%
> d. 70% to 80%

Distefano LJ, Blackburn JT, Marshall SW, Padua DA. *J Orthop Sports Phys Ther*. 2009;39(7):532-540.

41) Which of the following positions or activities will likely not result in pain due to hip impingement?

      a. Sumo squat
      b. Sitting with legs crossed
      c. "W" sitting
      d. Cycling

41) Which of the following positions or activities will likely not result in pain due to hip impingement?

  a. **Sumo squat**
  a. **Sumo squat will likely not result in hip impingement pain due to the abduction and external rotation associated with this movement. Exercises or positions that involved hip internal rotation, adduction, and flexion will likely cause pain.**
  b. Sitting with legs crossed
  c. "W" sitting
  d. Cycling

Emara K, Samir W, Motasem el H, Ghafar KA. Conservative treatment for mild femoroacetabular impingement. *J Orthop Surg*. 2011;19(1):41-45.

42) Regarding brachial plexus injuries, which of the following is a relative contraindication to return to play?

      a. Torg ratio <0.8 and asymptomatic
      b. Spina bifida occulta
      c. Prolonged symptomatic brachial plexus injury or transient quadriparesis >24 hours
      d. Asymptomatic clay shoveler's fracture

42) Regarding brachial plexus injuries, which of the following is a relative contraindication to return to play?

   a. Torg ratio <0.8 and asymptomatic
   b. Spina bifida occulta
   c. **Prolonged symptomatic brachial plexus injury or transient quadriparesis >24 hours**
      a. **Relative contraindications to return to play include:**
         i. **Prolonged symptomatic brachial plexus injury or transient quadriparesis greater than 24 hours**
         ii. **Greater to or equal than 3 prior episodes of stinger/burner**
         iii. **Status-post healed tow level anterior or posterior fusion surgery**
   d. Asymptomatic clay shoveler's fracture

Jeyamohan S, Harrop, Vaccaro AS, Sharan AD. Athletes returning to play after cervical spine or neurobrachial injury. *Curr Rev Musculoskelet Med*. 2008;1:175-179.

43) Persistent symptoms are generally reported in what percentage of concussions?

     a. 1%-5%
     b. 5%-10%
     c. 10%-15%
     d. 15%-20%

43) Persistent symptoms are generally reported in what percentage of concussions?

      a. 1%-5%
      b. 5%-10%
      c. 10%-15%
            a. Persistent symptoms are generally reported in 10%-15% of concussions. It is important for the persistently symptomatic concussion patient to be managed in a multidisciplinary manner.
      d. 15%-20%

McCrory P, Meeuwisse WH, Aubry M, et al. Consensus statement on concussion in sport: the 4th International Conference on Concussion in Sport held in Zurich, November 2012. *Br J Sports Med*. 2013;47:250-258.

44) The Child-SCAT 3 is most appropriate to assess a concussion in which of the following athletes?

      a. An 8-year-old gymnast
      b. A 13-year-old football player
      c. A 14-year-old rugby player
      d. A 16-year-old hockey player

5-12

44) The Child-SCAT 3 is most appropriate to assess a concussion in which of the following athletes?

      a. An 8-year-old gymnast
          a. The Child-SCAT 3 most appropriate to assess a concussion in pediatric athletes between the ages of 5 and 12.
      b. A 13-year-old football player
      c. A 14-year-old rugby player
      d. A 16-year-old hockey player

McCrory P, Meeuwisse WH, Aubry M, et al. Consensus statement on concussion in sport: the 4th International Conference on Concussion in Sport held in Zurich, November 2012. *Br J Sports Med.* 2013;47:250-258.

45) If an NCAA wrestler is on antibiotics for treatment of impetigo, folliculitis, or furuncles, how many hours does the athlete have to be on antibiotics to be declared eligible for competition?

 a. 24
 b. 48
 c. 72
 d. 96

45) If an NCAA wrestler is on antibiotics for treatment of impetigo, folliculitis, or furuncles, how many hours does the athlete have to be on antibiotics to be declared eligible for competition?

a. 24
b. 48
c. 72
      a. According to the NCAA Handbook "Wrestler must have completed 72 hours of antibiotic therapy and have no moist, exudative or draining lesions at meet or tournament time."
d. 96

National Collegiate Athletic Association. 2012–13 NCAA Sports Medicine Handbook. Indianapolis, IN; 2012.

46) During summer football conditioning, you note a defensive lineman becomes nauseated and starts vomiting following conditioning drills. He has an increased sweat rate and is complaining of a "pounding headache." You also note mild confusion. What heat-related illness is he most likely suffering from?

      a. Heat cramps
      b. Heat exhaustion
      c. Heat stroke
      d. Hyponatremia

46) During summer football conditioning, you note a defensive lineman becomes nauseated and starts vomiting following conditioning drills. He has an increased sweat rate and is complaining of a "pounding headache." You also note mild confusion. What heat-related illness is he most likely suffering from?

    a. Heat cramps
    b. Heat exhaustion
        a. According to the NATA, heat exhaustion is characterized by "fatigue, weakness, dizziness, headache, vomiting, nausea, lightheadedness, blood pressure, and impaired muscle coordination." Increased body temperature (<40.5°C), heavy sweating and dehydration are also affiliated with heat exhaustion.
    c. Heat stroke
    d. Hyponatremia

Casa DJ, DeMartini JK, Bergeron MF, et al. National Athletic Trainers' Association position statement: Exertional heat illnesses. *J Athl Train*. 2015;50(9):986-1000.

47) A clinician would suspect a lower motor neuron lesion of the hypoglossal nerve if the tongue deviates which direction?

        a. Away the injured side
        b. Toward the injured side
        c. Would roll
        d. Athlete would not be able to move tongue

47) A clinician would suspect a lower motor neuron lesion of the hypoglossal nerve if the tongue deviates which direction?

- a. Away the injured side
- **b. Toward the injured side**
    - **a. In the case of a lower motor neuron lesion, the tongue will be seen to deviate towards the injured side. This may accompanied with fasciculations and/or atrophy.**
- c. Would roll
- d. Athlete would not be able to move tongue

Mukherjee SK, Gowshami CB, Salam A, Kuddus R, Farazi MA, Baksh J. A case with unilateral hypoglossal nerve injury inbrachial cyst surgery. *J Brachial Plex Peripher Nerve Inj.* 2012;7(1):e26-e27.

48) What are the two main diagnostic criteria for exertional heat stroke?

    a. Central nervous system dysfunction and 105°F core body temperature
    b. Sweating cessation and 105°F core body temperature
    c. Dehydration and 105°F core body temperature
    d. Heart rate over 160 beats per minute and 105°F core body temperature

48) What are the two main diagnostic criteria for exertional heat stroke?

   a. **Central nervous system dysfunction and 105°F core body temperature**
      a. **The 2 main diagnostic criteria for exertional heat stroke are central nervous system (CNS) dysfunction and a core body temperature of 105°F. However, if an athlete exhibits CNS dysfunction and a 104°F temperature, it should be presumed that the athlete is suffering from exertional heat stroke.**
   b. Sweating cessation and 105°F core body temperature
   c. Dehydration and 105°F core body temperature
   d. Heart rate over 160 beats per minute and 105°F core body temperature

Casa DJ, DeMartini JK, Bergeron MF, et al. National Athletic Trainers' Association position statement: Exertional heat illnesses. *J Athl Train*. 2015;50(9):986-1000.

49) A male basketball player approaches you on the sideliners after "jamming" his finger during play. He reports tenderness of his right 4th digit and is unable to flex his DIP. You suspect the injury to be "Jersey Finger." What structure is involved in this injury?

      a. Central tendon slip
      b. Extensor digitorum tendon
      c. Flexor digitorum superficialis tendon
      d. Flexor digitorum profundus tendon

49) A male basketball player approaches you on the sideliners after "jamming" his finger during play. He reports tenderness of his right 4ᵗʰ digit and is unable to flex his DIP. You suspect the injury to be "Jersey Finger." What structure is involved in this injury?

       a. Central tendon slip
       b. Extensor digitorum tendon
       c. Flexor digitorum superficialis tendon
       d. **Flexor digitorum profundus tendon**
           a. **An avulsion injury of the flexor digitorum profundus tendon (jersey finger) results from a forced hyperextension of the distal interphalangeal joint while the finger is flexing actively. This injury most often occurs to the 4ᵗʰ digit.**

Ng CY, Hayton M. Management of acute hand injuries in athletes. *Orthop Trauma*. 2013;27(1):25-29.

50) You are providing medical coverage for a high school basketball tournament. An athlete approaches you reporting they "rolled" their ankle during the last game. A referral for radiographs to rule out a possible fracture would be necessary if the athlete presents with which of the following?

       a. Pain and tenderness over the sinus tarsi
       b. Pain and tenderness over the calcaneal tuberosity
       c. Pain and tenderness over the 2st metatarsal head
       d. Pain and tenderness over the base of the 5th metatarsal

50) You are providing medical coverage for a high school basketball tournament. An athlete approaches you reporting they "rolled" their ankle during the last game. A referral for radiographs to rule out a possible fracture would be necessary if the athlete presents with which of the following?

      a. Pain and tenderness over the sinus tarsi
      b. Pain and tenderness over the calcaneal tuberosity
      c. Pain and tenderness over the 2st metatarsal head
      d. Pain and tenderness over the base of the 5th metatarsal
            a. Applying the Ottawa ankle rules will dictate whether the athlete should be sent for radiographs. Pain and tenderness over the base of the 5th metatarsal is a positive finding of the Ottawa ankle rules.

Tiemstra JD. Update on acute ankle sprains. *Am Fam Physician.* 2012;85(12):1170-1176.

51) You are providing medical coverage for a local rugby tournament. An athlete is tackled around the knees and falls to the ground. A referral for radiographs to rule out a possible fracture would be necessary if the athlete presents with which of the following?

   a. The athlete complains of pain and tenderness over the pes anserine.
   b. The athlete complains of joint line knee pain
   c. The athlete complains of tenderness of the fibular head
   d. The athlete complains of pain over the tibial tuberosity

51) You are providing medical coverage for a local rugby tournament. An athlete is tackled around the knees and falls to the ground. A referral for radiographs to rule out a possible fracture would be necessary if the athlete presents with which of the following?

    a. The athlete complains of pain and tenderness over the pes anserine.
    b. The athlete complains of joint line knee pain
    c. The athlete complains of tenderness of the fibular head
        a. Applying the Ottawa knee rules will dictate whether the athlete should be sent for radiographs. Pain and tenderness over the fibular head is a positive finding of the Ottawa knee rules.
    b. The athlete complains of pain over the tibial tuberosity

Stiell IG, Greenberg GH, Wells GA, et al. Prospective validation of a decision rule for the use of radiography in acute knee injuries. *JAMA* 1996; 275:611-615.

52) You are providing medical coverage for a collegiate wrestling tournament. You evaluate an athlete who was thrown to the mat. Which of the following would warrant cervical stabilization and a referral for cervical radiographs?

     a. Headache
     b. Dizziness
     c. Midline cervical spine tenderness
     d. Ability to rotate neck 60° right and left

52) You are providing medical coverage for a collegiate wrestling tournament. You evaluate an athlete who was thrown to the mat. Which of the following would warrant cervical stabilization and a referral for cervical radiographs?

   a. Headache
   b. Dizziness
   c. Midline cervical spine tenderness
       a. Applying the Canadian cervical spine rules will dictate whether the athlete should be sent for radiographs. Midline cervical spine tenderness is a positive finding of the Canadian cervical spine rules.
   d. Ability to rotate neck 60° right and left

Stiell IG, Clement CM, McKnight RD, et al. The Canadian c-spine rule versus the NEXUS low-risk criteria in patients with trauma. *New Engl J Med*. 2003;349:2510-2518.

53) You are providing medical coverage for a collegiate hockey game. An athlete approaches you on the bench after taking a body check. Symptoms include increased heart rate, decreased blood pressure, and dry cough. Which of the following should you suspect?

      a. Hemothorax
      b. Diaphragmatic hernia
      c. Pneumothorax
      d. Aortic valve stenosis

53) You are providing medical coverage for a collegiate hockey game. An athlete approaches you on the bench after taking a body check. Symptoms include increased heart rate, decreased blood pressure, and dry cough. Which of the following should you suspect?

       a. Hemothorax
       b. Diaphragmatic hernia
       c. Pneumothorax
           a. Clinical features of pneumothorax include chest pain, breathlessness, reduced breath sounds, increased heart rate, decreased blood pressure, dry cough, and a tracheal shift towards the opposing side.
       d. Aortic valve stenosis

Currie GP, Alluri R, Christie GL, Legge JS. Pneumothorax: an update. *Postgrad Med J.* 2007;83:461-465.

54) A 22-year-old women's lacrosse player comes to you on the sidelines and is showing signs of exercise induced asthma. You measure her peak expiratory flow rate (PEF) on the sidelines and it is 12% below her baseline, what are the next appropriate management steps?

      a. Treat as a respiratory emergency
      b. Administer 2 puffs of short-acting β_2-agonist via metered dose inhaler with spacer
      c. Allow the athlete to return to play
      d. Administer high flow oxygen at 5 liters/minute

54) A 22-year-old women's lacrosse player comes to you on the sidelines and is showing signs of exercise induced asthma. You measure her peak expiratory flow rate (PEF) on the sidelines and it is 12% below her baseline, what are the next appropriate management steps?

    a. Treat as respiratory emergency
    b. Administer 2 puffs of short-acting β₂-agonist via metered dose inhaler with spacer
        a. After removing an athlete from play, the sports physical therapist should measure the athlete's peak expiratory flow (PEF) rate. If the PEF is 10%-15% below baseline, the sports physical therapist should administer 2 puffs of short acting β₂-agonist via metered dose inhaler with spacer. After 5 minutes, repeat PEF and if PEF has returned to baseline, athlete may return to play.
    c. Allow the athlete to return to play
    d. Administer high flow oxygen at 5 liters/minute

Miller MG, Weiler JM, Baker R, Collins J, D'Alonzo G. National Athletic Trainers' Association position statement: Management of asthma in athletes. . *J Athl Train*. 2005;40(3):224-245.

55) A high school hockey player gets hit in the stomach with a slap shot. After examination, you find that he has Kehr's sign. Which visceral organ is likely involved?

   a. Liver
   b. Gallbladder
   c. Appendix
   d. Spleen

55) A high school hockey player gets hit in the stomach with a slap shot. After examination, you find that he recently had the Epstein-Barr virus and also is positive for Kehr's sign. Which visceral organ is likely involved?

    a. Liver
    b. Gallbladder
    c. Appendix
    d. Spleen
        a. The Epstein-Barr virus commonly causes mononucleosis. Mononucleosis may cause an enlargement of the spleen and therefore, puts athletes at greater risk for splenic injury. Kehr's sign is referred pain to the tip of the left shoulder secondary to irritation of the diaphragm and is a classic symptom of a ruptured spleen.

Gannon EH, Howard T. Splenic injuries in athletes: a review; *Curr Sports Med Rep.* 2010;9(2):111-114.

56) A collegiate skier approaches you following a long day on the mountain. They report that they think they have superficial frostbite. Regarding rewarming, which of the following is not appropriate?

      a. Rewarming can occur at room temperature
      b. Rewarming can occur by placing frostbitten skin against warm skin
      c. Rewarming can be done by friction massage
      d. Rewarming water temperature should be between 98° F - 104° F

56) A collegiate skier approaches you following a long day on the mountain. They report that they think they have superficial frostbite. Regarding rewarming, which of the following is not appropriate?

    a. Rewarming can occur at room temperature
    b. Rewarming can occur by placing frostbitten skin against warm skin
    c. Rewarming can be done by friction massage
        a. Friction massage should be avoiding secondary to possibly causing additional tissue damage
    d. Rewarming water temperature should be between 98°F - 104°F

Cappaert TA, Stone JA, Castellani JW, Krause BA, Smith D, Stephens BA. National Athletic Trainers' Association position statement: Environmental cold injuries. *J Athl Train*. 2008;43(6):640-658.

57) A high school offensive lineman was injured during a play. You saw that the offensive lineman was weight-bearing on his forefoot and then someone landed on his heel causing an axial load. What type pathology are you suspecting from your observation of the injury?

     a. Lis Franc Injury
     b. Cuboid fracture
     c. High ankle sprain
     d. Freiberg infraction

57) A high school offensive lineman was injured during a play. You saw that the offensive lineman was weight-bearing on his forefoot and then someone landed on his heel causing an axial load. What type pathology are you suspecting from your observation of the injury?

  a. **Lis Franc Injury**
    a. **There are two main mechanisms of injury for Lis Franc injuries: forced hyperplantarflexion with a fix midfoot and when weight-bearing on the forefoot with an axial load through the heel.**
  b. Cuboid fracture
  c. High ankle sprain
  d. Freiberg infraction

Eleftheriou KI, Rosenfeld PT, Calder J. Lisfranc injuries: an update. *Knee Surg Sports Traumatol Arthrosc.* 2013;21:1434-1446.

58) According to the Ghent criteria, what would be a positive clinical diagnosis for Marfan Syndrome?

      a. A positive family history and involvement of 2 organ systems including 1 major criterion

      b. A negative family history and involvement of 2 organ systems including 1 major criterion

      c. A negative family history and major criterion from 2 systems and involvement of a 3rd system

      d. A and C only

58) According to the Ghent criteria, what would be a positive clinical diagnosis for Marfan Syndrome?

   a. A positive family history and involvement of 2 organ systems including 1 major criterion
   b. A negative family history and involvement of 2 organ systems including 1 major criterion
   c. A negative family history and major criterion from 2 systems and involvement of a 3rd system
   d. **A and C only**
      a. **The Ghent criteria was developed to help diagnose Marfan syndrome. In 2010, an international panel of experts has been revised. Cardinal features of the revised criteria include aortic root aneurysm and ectopia lentis.**

Loeys BL, Dietz HC, Braverman AC, et al. The revised Ghent nosology for the Marfan syndrome. *J Med Genet*. 2010;47:476-485.

59) What condition would automatically disqualify an athlete from participation?

  a. Bleeding disorder
  b. Atlantoaxial instability
  c. Cerebral palsy
  d. Carditis

59) What condition would automatically disqualify an athlete from participation?

    a. Bleeding disorder
    b. Atlantoaxial instability
    c. Cerebral palsy
    d. **Carditis**
        a. **If an athlete has the inflammation of the heart or carditis, they are automatically disqualified to participate in sport secondary to the possibility of carditis leading to sudden death with physical exertion.**

Rice, SG. Medical conditions affecting sports participation. *Pediatrics*. 2001;107(5);1205-1209.

60) You are treating a high school lineman for a SLAP tear mid-season. He asks you about his recent physical appointment where they perform numerous lab tests. The test results are as follows: Blood Pressure – 140/90 mmHg, triglycerides 170 mg/dL, fasting blood sugar 105 mg/dL and HDL 38 mg/dL. What is a possible diagnosis for this patient?

     a. Type I diabetes
     b. Type II diabetes
     c. Hypertension
     d. Metabolic syndrome

60) You are treating a high school lineman for a SLAP tear mid-season. He asks you about his recent physical appointment where they perform numerous lab tests. The test results are as follows: Blood Pressure – 140/90 mmHg, triglycerides 170 mg/dL, fasting blood sugar 105 mg/dL and HDL 38 mg/dL. What is a possible diagnosis for this patient?

    a. Type I diabetes
    b. Type II diabetes
    c. Hypertension
    d. Metabolic syndrome
        a. Having any 3 of the following 5 constitutes diagnosis of metabolic syndrome
           i. Elevated waist circumference
                1. ≥ 102 cm in men
                2. ≥ 88 cm in women
           ii. Elevated triglycerides
                1. ≥ 150 mg/dL (1.7 mmol/L)
                Or
                2. On drug treatment for elevated triglycerides
           iii. Reduced HDL-C
                1. <40 mg/dL (0.9 mmol/L) in men
                2. <50 mg/dL (1.1 mmol/L) in women
                Or
                3. On drug treatment for reduced HDL-C
           iv. Elevated blood pressure
                1. ≥130 mm Hg systolic blood pressure
                Or
                2. ≥ 85 mm Hg diastolic blood pressure
                Or
                3. On antihypertensive drug treatment in a patient with a history of hypertension
           v. Elevated fasting glucose
                1. ≥ 100 mg/dL

or
2. On drug treatment for elevated glucose

Grundy SM, Cleeman JI, Daniels SR, et al. Diagnosis and management of the metabolic syndrome. An American Heart Association/National Heart, Lung, and Blood Institute scientific statement. *Circulation*. 2005;112(17):2735-2752.

61) A 19-year-old softball player with type I diabetes comes to you during practice with obvious signs of mild hypoglycemia. You provide her with 10-15 grams of fast-acting carbohydrates and measure her blood glucose level after administration. 15 minutes later, you again measure her blood glucose level, which measures 60 mg/dL. What are your next steps?

    a. Let her return to play with serial blood glucose measurements
    b. Wait another 15 minutes and measure her blood glucose level again
    c. Administer another 10-15 grams of fast-acting carbohydrates and measure blood glucose levels
    d. Activate EMS immediately

61) A 19-year-old softball player with type I diabetes comes to you during practice with obvious signs of mild hypoglycemia. You provide her with 10-15 grams of fast-acting carbohydrates and measure her blood glucose level after administration. 15 minutes later, you again measure her blood glucose level, which measures 60 mg/dL. What are your next steps?

    a. Let her return to play with serial blood glucose measurements
    b. Wait another 15 minutes and measure her blood glucose level again
    c. Administer another 10-15 grams of fast-acting carbohydrates and measure blood glucose levels
        a. For an athlete who is showing signs of mild hypoglycemia you should administer 10g to 15g of fast-acting carbohydrates then measure their blood glucose level. Recheck blood glucose 15 minutes later. If blood glucose remains low, another 10g to 15g of fast-acting carbohydrates is warranted. Recheck blood glucose levels in 15 minutes. If blood glucose is has not returned to normal values, activate the emergency medical system.
    d. Activate EMS immediately

Jimenez CC, Corcoran MH, Crawley JT, et al. National Athletic Trainers' Association position statement: Management of the athlete with type 1 diabetes mellitus. *J Athl Train*. 2007;42(4):536-545.

62) A 16 year-old high school shot put athlete with a history of scoliosis is complaining of thoracic back pain that increases with the throwing motion during practice and competition. No history of a traumatic event or neurological symptoms. What is the most likely diagnosis?

       a. Slipped vertebral apophysis
       b. Acute leukemia
       c. Scheurmann's disease
       d. Discitis

62) A 16 year-old high school shot put athlete with a history of scoliosis is complaining of thoracic back pain that increases with the throwing motion during practice and competition. No history of a traumatic event or neurological symptoms. What is the most likely diagnosis?

  a. Slipped vertebral apophysis
  b. Acute leukemia
  c. **Scheuermann's disease**
      a. **Scheuermann's disease is described by painful, fix kyphosis that most commonly occurs in teenagers. Clinical symptoms include pain worsened by vertebral rotation, flexion, and extension, muscular spasms, back pain and limited flexibility. Scoliosis is associated with Scheurmann's disease in 15% - 20% of cases.**
  d. Discitis

Palazzo, C, Sailhan F, Revel M. Scheuermann's disease: an update. *Joint Bone Spine*. 2014;81:209-214.

63) You are traveling with a group of climbers on a trip to a local mountain. During the second day of the ascent, you note that one of your climbers has developed acute mountain sickness. If this climber has a a headache, which of the following symptoms would the climber have to have to be considered to be suffering from acute mountain sickness?

       a. Decreased heart rate
       b. Loss of appetite
       c. Blurry vision
       d. Difficulty to wake when sleeping

63) You are traveling with a group of climbers on a trip to a local mountain. During the second day of the ascent, you note that one of your climbers has developed acute mountain sickness. If this climber has a a headache, which of the following symptoms would the climber have to have to be considered to be suffering from acute mountain sickness?

    a. Decreased heart rate
    b. Loss of appetite
        a. According to the Lake Louise Consensus on the Definition and Quantification of Altitude Illness, acute mountain sickness is defined as an individual having a high-altitude-related headache plus one or more of the following symptoms: loss of appetite, nausea, or vomiting, fatigue or weakness, dizziness or lightheadedness, or difficulty sleeping.
    c. Blurry vision
    d. Difficulty to wake when sleeping

DeWeber K, Scorza K. Return to activity at altitude after high-altitude illness. *Sports Health*. 2010;2(4):291-300.

64) What condition is an individual considered to have when they have a lateral curve of the spine on the frontal plane which is greater than 10° when measured on radiographs using the Cobb method?

       a. Vertebral lateral shift
       b. Scoliosis
       c. Lumbar kyphosis
       d. Scheurmann's kyphosis

64) What condition is an individual considered to have when they have a lateral curve of the spine on the frontal plane which is greater than 10° when measured on radiographs using the Cobb method?

    a. Vertebral lateral shift
    b. Scoliosis
        a. Scoliosis is characterized by a lateral curvature in the spine in the frontal plane and measures greater than 10° using the Cobb method. Scoliosis also includes lateral vertebral body rotation and tilting across the apex toward the convexity of the curve in the axial plane.
    c. Lumbar kyphosis
    d. Scheurmann's kyphosis

Suk A, Tsirikos AI. Current concepts and controversies on adolescent idiopathic scoliosis: part I. *Indian J Orthop*. 2013;47(2):117-128.

65) You are working with a high school football team during preseason camp. Upon review of team medical records, you note that one of the new athletes has sickle cell trait. What should this athlete's participation status be?

       a. Cleared with no monitoring needed
       b. Cleared with monitoring for heat- and dehydration conditions
       c. Not cleared due to risk of heat- and dehydration conditions
       d. Disqualified due to sickle cell trait

65) You are working with a high school football team during preseason camp. Upon review of team medical records, you note that one of the new athletes has sickle cell trait. What should this athlete's participation status be?

    a. Cleared with no monitoring needed
    b. Cleared with monitoring for heat- and dehydration conditions
        a. For individuals with sickle cell trait, there are no contraindications for athletic participation. Additionally, athletes who are found to have sickle cell trait should be educated and monitored closely for heat and dehydration conditions.
    c. Not cleared due to risk of heat- and dehydration conditions
    d. Disqualified due to sickle cell trait

Rice, SG. Medical conditions affecting sports participation. *Pediatrics*. 2001;107(5);1205-1209.

66) You have been working with a rugby athlete who has had a significant history of recurrent shoulder dislocations. An orthopedic surgeon has suggested performing a Latarjet procedure to prevent further dislocations. This procedure involves removal of a section of what bone and that bones reattachment to the glenoid?

  a. Coracoid process
  b. Clavicle
  c. Greater tubercle of the humerus
  d. Spine of the scapula

66) You have been working with a rugby athlete who has had a significant history of recurrent shoulder dislocations. An orthopedic surgeon has suggested performing a Latarjet procedure to prevent further dislocations. This procedure involves removal of a section of what bone and that bones reattachment to the glenoid?

    a. Coracoid process
        a. The Latarjet procedure is an operation that involves transfering a coracoid process to the anteior glenoid to prevent further reccurance of anterior dislocation of the humeral head.
    b. Clavicle
    c. Greater tubercle of the humerus
    d. Spine of the scapula

Schmid SL, Farshad M, Catanzaro S, Gerber C. The latarjet procedure for the treatment of recurrence of anterior instability of the shoulder after operative repair. *J Bone Joint Surg Am*. 2012;94(11):e75.

67) Of the following exercises, which one should be avoided by women who are pregnant?

      a. Running
      b. Backstroke
      c. Cycling
      d. Step aerobics

67) Of the following exercises, which one should be avoided by women who are pregnant?

    a. Running
    b. Backstroke
        a. Backstroke should be avoided due to the being supine for a prolonged period of time. The supine position compresses the inferior vena cava which restricts venous return, reduces ejection fracture, reduces cardiaco output, and reduces uterine perfusion. This can have negative effects on the developing fetus.
    c. Cycling
    d. Step aerobics

O'Brien LM, Warland J. Typical sleep positions in preganant women. *Early Hum Dev*. 2014;90(6):315-317.

68) You are assisting with pre-participation examinations for a high school. During a disordered eating screen, a senior female athlete reports she is only have 7 mentrual cycles per year. What would this be considered?

    a. Primary amenorrhea
    b. Secondary amenorrhea
    c. Eumenorrhea
    d. Oligomenorrhea

68) You are assisting with pre-participation examinations for a high school. During a disordered eating screen, a senior female athlete reports she is only have 7 mentrual cycles per year. What would this be considered?

  a. Primary amenorrhea
  b. Secondary amenorrhea
  c. Eumenorrhea
  d. Oligomenorrhea
      a. Oligomenorrhea is defined as a female having fewer than 9 mentual cycles per year. Mentural irregularies may be concerning secondary to their direct relationship with body mass density.

Chu SM, Gustafson KE, Leiszler M. Female athlete triad: clinical evluation and treatment. *Am J Lifestyle* Med. 2013; 7(6):387-394.

69) A 19-year-old male cross fitter complains of left groin pain. He reports that it intensifies during cutting and jumping type movements. He adds that the pain increases when he does any lifting. He demonstrates normal hip range of motion and strength in all motions however, resisted hip motions all result in groin pain. Palpation reveals tenderness over the inguinal ligament. What is the most likely diagnosis?

     a. Sports hernia
     b. Testicular torsion
     c. Femoral acetabular impingement
     d. Adductor strain

69) A 19-year-old male cross fitter complains of left groin pain. He reports that it intensifies during cutting and jumping type movements. He adds that the pain increases when he does any lifting. He demonstrates normal hip range of motion and strength in all motions however, resisted hip motions all result in groin pain. Palpation reveals tenderness over the inguinal ligament. What is the most likely diagnosis?

   a. Sports hernia
       a. Sports hernia is described as a weakness in the posterior inguinal wall that results in a hernia. Sport hernias commonly occur in soccer, hockey, and football athletes. Patient may describe groin pain after activity that subsides with rest. Clinical presentation can include tenderness with palpation over the addominal region, inguinal ligament, pubic tubercle, pubic symphasis, and adductor musculature.
   b. Testicular torsion
   c. Femoral acetabular impingement
   d. Adductor strain

Woodward JS, Parker A, MacDonald RM. Non-surgical treatment of a professional hockey player with the signs and symptoms of sports hernia: a case report. *Int J Sports Phys Ther*. 2012;7(1):85-100.

70) Following anterior cervical discetomy and fusion, nerve palsy is most common in what nerve?

  a. Long thoracic nerve
  b. Dorsal scapular nerve
  c. Recurrent laryngeal nerve
  d. Phrenic nerve

70) Following anterior cervical discetomy and fusion, nerve palsy is most common in what nerve?

    a. Long thoracic nerve
    b. Dorsal scapular nerve
    c. Recurrent laryngeal nerve
        a. Unilateral recurrent laryngeal nerve palsy is a common complication following cervical surgery. The patient will have hoarseness and voice weakness.
    d. Phrenic nerve

Fountas KN, Kapsalaki EZ, Nikolakakos LG, et al. Anterior cervical discectomy and fusion associated complications. *Spine*. 2007;32(21):2310-2317.

71) A 10-year-old female presents to the clinic with persistent swelling of her knee and ankle. No known injury. She reports she is not participating in gymnastics anymore secondary to discomfort. She also states that she has joint stiffness in the morning that improves throughout the day. What is her most likely diagnosis?

      a. Juvenile rheumatoid arthritis
      b. Chronic ankle sprain
      c. Sever's disease
      d. Frieberg's disease

71) A 10-year-old female presents to the clinic with persistent swelling of her knee and ankle. No known injury. She reports she is not participating in gymnastics anymore secondary to discomfort. She also states that she has joint stiffness in the morning that improves throughout the day. What is her most likely diagnosis?

    a. Juvenile rheumatoid arthritis
        a. Juvenile rheumatoid arthritis is the most common type of arthritis in children under 17 years of age. Most commonly, juvenile rheumatoid arthritis occurs in females. Etiology of this condition is unknown. Clinical presentation will include persistent swelling of joints, lethargy, and stiffness that is more apparent in the morning. The patient may also report decreased physical activity and flu-like symptoms.
    b. Chronic ankle sprain.
    c. Sever's disease
    d. Frieberg's disease

Weiss JE, Ilowite NT. Juvenile idiopathic arthritis". *Pediatr Clin North Am.* 2005;52(2):413-442.

72) An athlete suffered a brachial plexus injury and now presents with partial ptosis, miosis, and anhidrosis. What condition may this athlete be suffering from?

    a. Horner syndrome
    b. Third nerve palsy
    c. Argyll Robertson pupil
    d. Raccoon eyes

72) An athlete suffered a brachial plexus injury and now presents with partial ptosis, paradoxical contralateral eyelid retraction, and aniscoria. What condition may this athlete be suffering from?

   a. **Horner syndrome**
      a. **Horner syndrome is a condition in which the sympathetic nerve supply to the eye is disrupted. Common causes of Horner syndrome may include primary neuron lesion, Pancoast tumor or infection of the lung apex, lesion of the postganglionic neuron, migraine, and trama to the brachial plexus. Clinical presentation may include ptosis, anhidrosis, miosis, and anisocoria.**
   b. Third nerve palsy
   c. Argyll Robertson pupil
   d. Raccoon eyes

Reede DL, Garcon E, Smoker WR, Kardon R. Horner's syndrome: clinical and radiographic evaluation. Neuroimaging Clin N Am. 2008. 18(2):369-85.

73) An ice hockey player you are working with has a history of groin strains. You are focusing your strength training on hip adductors and hip abductor to prevent further groin strains. The best predictor of a future groin strain is an adductor-to-abductor strength ratio less than what percent?

       a. 90%
       b. 85%
       c. 80%
       d. 75%

73) An ice hockey player you are working with has a history of groin strains. You are focusing your strength training on hip adductors and hip abductor to prevent further groin strains. The predictor of a future groin strain is an adductor-to-abductor strength ratio less than what percent?

   a. 90%
   b. 85%
   c. 80%
      a. **Hip adductors-to-abductors strength ratio greater than 80% can lower the incidence of hip adductor muscle strains. A ratio below 80% is a predictor of future groin strains.**
   d. 75%

Tyler TF, Nicholas SJ, Campbell RJ, Donellan S, McHugh MP. The effectiveness of a preseason exercise program to prevent adductor muscle strains in professional ice hockey players. *Am J Sports Med*. 2002;30(5):680-683.

74) You are performing a running gait analysis on a middle-aged recreational runner. Prior to the running gait analysis, you take a history from the athlete. From the given history, you are concerned that this athlete is at risk for a stress fracture. Which of the following is not a risk factor for stress fracture?

       a. Sudden increase in physical activity
       b. Female sex
       c. Consuming more than 10 alcoholic drinks per week
       d. High levels of 25-hydroxyvitamin D

74) You are performing a running gait analysis on a middle-aged recreational runner. Prior to the running gait analysis, you take a history from the athlete. From the given history, you are concerned that this athlete is at risk for a stress fracture. Which of the following is not a risk factor for stress fracture?

      a. Sudden increase in physical activity
      b. Female sex
      c. Consuming more than 10 alcoholic drinks per week
      d. High levels of 25-hydroxyvitamin D
            a. The follow are considered risk factors for stress fractures: consuming more than 10 alcoholic drinks per week, excessive physical activity with limited rest periods, female athlete triad, female sex, low levels of 25-hydroxyvitamin D, recreational running (more than 25 miles per week), smoking, sudden increase in physical activity, and participating in track or running sports.

Patel DS, Roth M, Kapil N. Stress fractures: diagnosis, treatment, and prevention. *Am Fam Phys*. 2011;83(1):39-46.

75) In youth baseball pitchers, what risk factor has the strongest correlation to injury?

        a. Amount of pitches thrown
        b. Type of pitches thrown
        c. Velocity of pitches thrown
        d. Poor pitching mechanics

75) In youth baseball pitchers, what risk factor has the strongest correlation to injury?

>   **a. Amount of pitches thrown**
>   >   a. **The risk factor with the strongest correlation to injury is the amount of pitching that occurs. Due to this relationship, numerous organizations provide guidelines for pitch count and rest day guidelines.**
>   b. Type of pitches thrown
>   c. Velocity of pitches thrown
>   d. Poor pitching mechanics

Olsen SJ, Fleisig GS, Dun S, Loftice J, Andrews JR. Risk factors for shoulder and elbow injuries in adolescent baseball pitchers. Am J Sports Med. 2006;34:905-912.

76) Which interventions is not supported in the prevention of ankle injury?

        a. Improved neuromuscular control
        b. Improved strength of lower leg musculature
        c. Correct dorsiflexion range of motion deficits
        d. Improved strength of hip adductors

76) Which interventions is not supported in the prevention of ankle injury?

      a. Improved neuromuscular control
      b. Improved strength of lower leg muscular
      c. Correct dorsiflexion range of motion deficits
      d. Improved strength of hip adductors
            a. According to the National Athletic Trainers' Association, improving neuromuscular control, lower leg muscular strength, and correcting dorsiflexion range of motion deficits have been suggested to assist in prevention of ankle injury.

Kaminski TW, Hertel J, Amendola N, Docherty CL, Dolan MG, Hopkins JT, et al. National Athletic Trainers' Association position statement: conservative management and prevention of ankle sprains in athletes. *J Athl Train*. 2013;48(4):528-545.

77) According to the NCAA, which of the following is not a mandatory piece of equipment for football?

        a. Hip pads with tailbone protector
        b. Knee pads
        c. Intra-oral mouthpiece in visible color
        d. Abdominal protector

77) According to the NCAA, which of the following is not a mandatory piece of equipment for football?

     a. Hip pads with tailbone protector
     b. Knee pads
     c. Intra-oral mouthpiece in visible color
     d. Abdominal protector
          a. According to the NCAA, the mandatory equipment to participate in football include soft knee pads (>1/2 inch), face masks and helmets (4 or 6 point chin strap), shoulder pads, hip pad with tailbone protector, knee pads, and intra-oral mouthpiece in visible color (covers all upper teeth). No pad or protective equipment are allowed outside of pants.

NCAA. Football 2016 and 2017 Rules and Interpretation. Indianapolis, IN, 2016.

78) According to the NCAA, what is the minimum wire gauge of a mesh mask for a fencer?

       a. 0.5 millimeters diameter
       b. 1.0 millimeters diameter
       c. 1.5 millimeters diameter
       d. 2.0 millimeters diameter

78) According to the NCAA, what is the minimum wire gauge of a mesh mask for a fencer?

      a. 0.5 millimeters diameter
      b. 1.0 millimeters diameter
          a. The NCAA requires that there be a minimum gauge diameter of 1 millimeter for wire mesh fencing masks.
      c. 1.5 millimeters diameter
      d. 2.0 millimeters diameter

NCAA. 2014-2015 NCAA Sports Medicine Handbook. Indianapolis, IN, 2014.

79) What is the maximum amount of recommended hours of vigorous physical activity to prevent pediatric injuries?

       a. 6-10
       b. 12-15
       c. 16-20
       d. 22-25

79) What is the maximum amount of recommended hours of vigorous physical activity to prevent pediatric injuries?

    a. 6-10
    b. 12-15
    c. 16-20
        a. A general guideline of a maximum of 16-20 hours of vigorous physical activities is recommended to prevent pediatric injury.
    d. 22-25

Valovich McLeod TC, Decoster LC, Loud KJ, et al. National athletic trainers' association position statement: prevention of pediatric overuse injuries. *J Athl Train*. 2011;46(2):206-220.

80) Which is not a type of mouth guard?

     a. Custom-fabricated mouth guard
     b. Mouth-formed mouth guard
     c. Stock mouth guard
     d. Gel forming mouth guard

80) Which is not a type of mouth guard?

    a. Custom-fabricated mouth guard
    b. Mouth-formed mouth guard
    c. Stock mouth guard
    d. Gel forming mouth guard
        a. The American Society for Testing and Materials classifies mouth guards into three categories. These include custom-fabricated mouth guards, mouth-formed or boi-and-bite mouth guards, and stock mouth guards.

Newsome PR, Tran DC, Cooke MS. The role of the mouthguard in the prevention of sports-related dental injuries: a review. *Int J Paediatr Dent*. 2001;11:396-404.

81) Pain and injuries are significantly decreased on what type of tennis playing surface?

        a. Asphalt/concrete
        b. Felt carpet
        c. Synthetic grass
        d. Clay

81) Pain and injuries are significantly decreased on what type of tennis playing surface?

   a. Asphalt/concrete
   b. Felt carpet
   c. Synthetic grass
   d. Clay
         a. Tennis playing surfaces that allowed the athlete to slide, such as clay, were found to have significantly fewer injuries compared to playing surfaces that do not allow sliding.

Dragoo JL, Braun HJ. The effect of playing surface on injury rate: a review of the current literature. *Sports Med*. 2010;40(11):981-990.

82) What is the single most important method in athletics for prevention of the transmission of community acquired - methicillin-resistant Staphylococcus aureus?

       a. Avoid sharing towels
       b. Hand washing
       c. Cover skin lesions before participation
       d. Maintain clean facilities and equipment

82) What is the single most important method in athletics for prevention of the transmission of community acquired - methicillin-resistant Staphylococcus aureus?

   a. Avoid sharing towels
   b. Hand washing
      a. According to the Centers for Disease Control, hand washing is the single most important prevention strategy for the transmission of community acquired - methicillin-resistant Staphylococcus aureus. Hands should be washed with soap and warm water or alcohol-based hand sanitizer.
   c. Cover skin lesions before participation
   d. Maintain clean facilities and equipment

Centers for Disease Control and Prevention. Methicillin resistant staphylococcus aureus infections among competitive sports participants- Colorado, Indiana, Pennsylvania, and Los Angeles County. *Morb Mortal Wkly* Rep. 2003;52:793–795.

83) You are working with a collegiate football team. The coaches ask you your advice on heat acclimation for pre-season practices. They want your recommendation on when to go 100% live with contact drills. Your recommendation should be what?

        a. No earlier than day 4
        b. No earlier than day 5
        c. No earlier than day 6
        d. No earlier than day 7

83) You are working with a high school football team. The coaches ask you your advice on heat acclimation for pre-season practices. They want your recommendation on when to go 100% live with contact drills. Your recommendation should be what?

- a. No earlier than day 4
- b. No earlier than day 5
- **c. No earlier than day 6**
  - **a. On heat acclimatization days 3-5 for football athletes, contact with blocking sleds and tackling dummies may begin. No sooner than day 6 may thee be 100% live contact drills.**
- d. No earlier than day 7

Armstrong LE, Baker LB, Bergeron M, et al. Preseason heat-acclimatization guidelines for secondary school athletics. *J Athl Train*. 2009;44(3):332-333.

84) You are providing coverage for a high school field hockey match when the weather turns poorly. Lightning is seen and play is suspended. How much time much elapse with no new lightning strikes or hearing of thunder before play may resume?

        a. 10 minutes
        b. 15 minutes
        c. 30 minutes
        d. 60 minutes

84) You are providing coverage for a high school field hockey match when the weather turns poorly. Lightning is seen and play is suspended. How much time much elapse with no new lightning strikes or hearing of thunder before play may resume?

      a. 10 minutes
      b. 15 minutes
      c. 30 minutes
            a. All activities should be suspended for at least 30 minutes from the last lightning strike seen (or at least 4 nautical miles away) and after the last audible thunder. The clock will restart at 30 minutes after each new lightning strike within 5 nautical miles or each time thunder is heard.
      b. 60 minutes

Walsh KM, Cooper M, Holle R, et al. National Athletic Trainers' Association position statement: Lightning safety for athletics and recreation. *J Athl Train*. 2013;48(1):258-270.

85) What is the earliest age an adolescent pitcher is recommended to start throwing curveballs?

  a. 10 years old
  b. 12 years old
  c. 14 years old
  d. 16 years old

85) What is the earliest age an adolescent pitcher is recommended to start throwing curveballs?

      a. 10 years old
      b. 12 years old
      c. 14 years old
            a. The earliest recommended age that adolescent pitchers may begin throwing curveballs is 14. The curveball was found to have elbow and shoulder pain in youth pitchers. Additionally, to properly throw a curveball, a new set of mechanics must be learned that may increase loads on the pitchers elbow and shoulder.
      d. 16 years old

Petty DH, Andrews JR, Fleisig GS, Cain EL. Ulnar collateral ligament reconstruction in high school baseball players: clinical results and injury risk factors. *Am J Sports Med*. 2004;32(5):1158-1164.

86) The 3-pronged approach to preventing hypoglycemia relies on all of the following except…

a. Frequent blood glucose monitoring
b. Carbohydrate supplementation
c. Insulin adjustments
d. Temperature monitoring

86) The 3-pronged approach to preventing hypoglycemia relies on all of the following except…

    a. Frequent blood glucose monitoring
    b. Carbohydrate supplementation
    c. Insulin adjustments
    d. Temperature monitoring
        a. **The 3-pronged approach to preventing hypoglycemia involves blood glucose monitoring, carbohydrate supplementation, and insulin adjustments. Blood glucose levels should be checked 2-3 times before activity, every 30 minutes during activity, and up to 4 hours after exercise. Carbohydrates should be consumed before, during, and after activity. The quantity of carbohydrate consumed depends on blood glucose levels. Insulin adjustments may be needed depending on blood glucose levels, insulin delivery method, and exercise intensity.**

Casa DJ, Guskiewicz KM, Anderson SA, et al. National Athletic Trainers' Association position statement: preventing sudden death in sports. *J Athl Train*. 2012;47(1):96-118.

87) Wrestlers who have demonstrated a predisposition for tinea corporis during the competitive season have been successfully treated prophylactically during the season with a…

      a. High dosage of fluconazole
      b. Low dosage of fluconazole
      c. High dosage of valacyclovir
      d. Low dosage of valacyclovir

87) Wrestlers who have demonstrated a predisposition for tinea corporis during the competitive season have been successfully treated prophylactically during the season with a…

a. High dosage of fluconazole
b. Low dosage of fluconazole
  a. Wrestlers have successfully been treated prophylactically during the season for tinea corporis with a low dosage of fluconazole. Dosage and frequency include 150 mg every other week or 200 mg per month.
c. High dosage of valacyclovir
d. Low dosage of valacyclovir

Zinder SM, Basler RS, Foley J, Scarlata C, Vasily DB. National Athletic Trainers' Association position statement: skin diseases. 2010;45(4):411-428.

88) A Division I collegiate hockey player has been participating in dry land training focusing on lower extremity plyometric exercises. He is concerned about the amount of rest period he gets between sets. What are your recommendations for this athlete in regards to work-to-rest ratio?

        a. 1:1 to 1:2
        b. 1:3 to 1:4
        c. 1:5 to 1:10
        d. 1:15 to 1:20

88) A Division I collegiate hockey player has been participating in dry land training focusing on lower extremity plyometric exercises. He is concerned about the amount of rest period he gets between sets. What are your recommendations for this athlete in regards to work-to-rest ratio?

    a. 1:1 to 1:2
    b. 1:3 to 1:4
    c. 1:5 to 1:10
        a. A rest ratio of 1:5 to 1:10 allows for appropriate performance of the plyometric exercise. High intensity plyometric exercises depend heavily on the phosphagen and anaerobic energy systems. If recovery periods are too short, these systems have difficulty developing their efficiency and effectiveness.
    d. 1:15 to 1:20

Potach DH, Chu DA. Plyometric training. In: Baechle TR, Earle RW, eds. *Essentials of Strength and Conditioning.* 3rd ed. Champaign, IL: Human Kinetics; 2008:414-456.

89) A collegiate football athlete approaches you regarding strength training for his core exercises during the strength/power phase prior to transitioning into the competitive season. What is the most appropriate volume for his resistance training at this time?

        a. 3-6 sets, 10-20 repetitions
        b. 2-5 sets, 4-8 repetitions
        c. 1-3 sets, 1-3 repetitions
        d. 3-5 sets, 2-5 repetitions

89) A collegiate football athlete approaches you regarding strength training for his core exercises during the power phase prior to transitioning into the competitive season. Regarding a multiple-effort event, what is the most appropriate volume for his resistance training?

  a. 3-6 sets, 10-20 repetitions
  b. 2-5 sets, 4-8 repetitions
  c. 1-3 sets, 1-3 repetitions
  d. 3-5 sets, 3-5 repetitions
    a. **During the strength/power phase, the volume is low with recommended 3-5 sets of 3-5 repetitions each. Power exercise volume is lower than strength exercises due to fewer repetitions and decreased loads to optimize the quality of the exercise.**

Baechle TR, Earle RW, Wathen D. Resistance Training. In: Baechle TR, Earle RW, eds. *Essentials of Strength and Conditioning.* 3rd ed. Champaign, IL: Human Kinetics; 2008:382-412.

90) You are working with a high school women's lacrosse player following anterior cruciate ligament reconstruction. You decide you are going to test her agility using a standardized test. Which of the following would not be an appropriate test?

    a. T-test
    b. Hexagon test
    c. 40 yard dash
    d. 5-10-5 shuttle

90) You are working with a high school women's lacrosse player following anterior cruciate ligament reconstruction. You decide you are going to test her agility using a standardized test. Which of the following would not be an appropriate test?

    a. T-test
    b. Hexagon test
    c. 40 yard dash
        a. The 40 yard dash is considered a speed test and not an agility test. An agility test will test an athlete's overall coordinative abilities.
    d. 5-10-5 shuttle

Harman E, Garhammer J. Administration, Scoring, and Interpretation of Selected Tests. In: Baechle TR, Earle RW, eds. *Essentials of Strength and Conditioning.* 3rd ed. Champaign, IL: Human Kinetics; 2008:382-412.

91) You are working with a collegiate hockey player in the late stages of rehabilitation following a grade I hamstring strain. You want to initiate plyometric exercises to promote power. How many foot contacts would be appropriate at this time?

        a. 80-100 foot contacts
        b. 100-120 foot contacts
        c. 120-140 foot contacts
        d. 140-160 foot contacts

91) You are working with a collegiate hockey player in the late stages of rehabilitation following a grade I hamstring strain. You want to initiate plyometric exercises to promote power. How many foot contacts would be appropriate at this time?

> **a. 80-100 foot contacts**
> > **a. Recommended foot contacts for a beginner or someone with no experience is 80-100 foot contacts. Too many foot contacts for a beginner may cause musculoskeletal injury.**
> b. 100-120 foot contacts
> c. 120-140 foot contacts
> d. 140-160 foot contacts

Potach DH, Chu DA. Plyometric training. In: Baechle TR, Earle RW, eds. *Essentials of Strength and Conditioning.* 3rd ed. Champaign, IL: Human Kinetics; 2008:414-456.

92) A collegiate male soccer athlete is conditioning during early winter. He has a noticed a decrease in his aerobic power during a functional test. A decrease in aerobic power is first seen at what percent of body weight loss secondary to dehydration?

    a. 1-2%
    b. 3-4%
    c. 5%
    d. 6%

92) A collegiate male soccer athlete is conditioning during early winter. He has a noticed a decrease in his aerobic power during a functional test. A decrease in aerobic power is first seen at what percent of body weight loss secondary to dehydration?

     a. 1-2%
          a. Dehydration of 1% to 2% of body weight in a cool environment will cause a decrease in aerobic power.
     b. 3-4%
     c. 5%
     d. 6%

Casa DJ, Armstrong LE, Hillman SK, et al. National Athletic Trainers' Association position statement: Fluid replacement for athletes. *J Athl Train*. 2000;35(2):212-224.

93) A triathlete approaches you for your advice regarding fluid replacement during the bike portion of her next race. What is the recommended maximum carbohydrate concentration of the beverage?

      a. 4%
      b. 6%
      c. 8%
      d. 10%

93) A triathlete approaches you for your advice regarding fluid replacement during the bike portion of her next race. What is the recommended maximum carbohydrate concentration of the beverage?

    a. 4%
    b. 6%
    c. 8%
        a. If utilizing a single beverage for both fluid replacement and carbohydrate delivery, the recommended maximum carbohydrate concentration is 8%. A high percent carbohydrate concentration will reduce gastric emptying and may cause nausea.
    d. 10%

Rodriguez NR, DiMarco NM, Langley S. Nutrition and athletic performance. *Med Sci Sports Exerc*. 2009;41(3):709-731.

94) A male football player reports to you that he has been using anabolic steroids to try and get an "edge" on his competition. Which of the following is not a potential health effects associated with anabolic steroid abuse?

      a. Decreased antibody synthesis
      b. Increased likelihood of temporomandibular dysfunction
      c. Increased total cholesterol
      d. Increased high-density lipoproteins

94) A male football player reports to you that he has been using anabolic steroids to try and get an "edge" on his competition. Which of the following is not a potential health effects associated with anabolic steroid abuse?

    a. Decreased antibody synthesis
    b. Increased likelihood of temporomandibular dysfunction
    c. Increased total cholesterol
    d. Increased high-density lipoproteins
        a. Anabolic steroid use is associated with decreased high-density lipoproteins. The associated lipid profile with anabolic steroid use is risk factor for coronary heart disease.

Kersey RD, Elliot DL, Goldberg L, et al. National Athletic Trainers' Association position statement: Anabolic-androgenic steroids. *J Athl Train*. 2012;47(5):567-588.

95) According to the National Collegiate Athletic Association (NCAA), what type of nutritional supplement can be provided to the student-athletic by an athletic department for the purpose of providing additional calories and electrolytes?

a. Permissible
b. Authorized
c. Sanctioned
d. Allowable

95) According to the National Collegiate Athletic Association (NCAA), what type of nutritional supplement can be provided to the student-athletic by an athletic department for the purpose of providing additional calories and electrolytes?

   a. Permissible
   - **a. Permissible supplements are allowed to be given to collegiate student-athletes to supplement calories and electrolytes. Permissible nutritional supplements are distinctive from NCAA banned supplements.**
   b. Authorized
   c. Sanctioned
   d. Allowable

Buell JL, Franks R, Ransone J, Powers ME, Laquale KM, Carlson-Phillips A. National Athletic Trainers' Association position statement: Evaluation of dietary supplements for performance nutrition. *J Athl Train*. 2013;48(1):124-136.

96) A high school football athlete wants to train and diet throughout the summer to lose weight. He approaches you and asks your recommendations on an appropriate weight loss rate. What is your recommendation?

      a. 1-2 pounds per week
      b. 3-4 pounds per week
      c. 5-6 pounds per week
      d. 7-8 pounds per week

96) A high school football athlete wants to train and diet throughout the summer to lose weight. He approaches you and asks your recommendations on an appropriate weight loss rate. What is your recommendation?

    a. **1-2 pounds per week**
        a. **On average, an athlete should not exceed weight loss of more than 1-2 pounds per week secondary to dehydration risk and potential for unhealthy behaviors.**
    b. 3-4 pounds per week
    c. 5-6 pounds per week
    d. 7-8 pounds per week

Turocy PS, DePalma BF, Hroswill CA. National Athletic Trainers' Association position statement: Safe weight loss and maintenance practices in sport and exercise. *J Athl Train*. 2011;46(3):322-336.

97) Regarding strength training for adolescents, which of the following is not true?

   a. Adolescents should avoid power lifting until they reach skeletal maturity
   b. Level arms on weight machines may not be appropriately sized for adolescents
   c. Free weight exercises increases likelihood of injury secondary to underdeveloped coordination
   d. Strength training in adolescents is not effective due to lower levels of circulating testosterone.

97) Regarding strength training for adolescents, which of the following is not true?

    a. Adolescents should avoid power lifting until they reach skeletal maturity

    b. Level arms on weight machines may not be appropriately sized for adolescents

    c. Free weight exercises increases likelihood of injury secondary to underdeveloped coordination

    d. Strength training in adolescents is not effective due to lower levels of circulating testosterone.

        a. Numerous studies have demonstrated an increase in adolescent strength following completing a strength training program. Strength training in children is hypothesized to increase the number and coordination of motor during in addition to the firing rate.

Dahab KS, McCambridge TM. Strength training in children and adolescents. *Sports Health*. 2009;1(13):223-226.

98) At minimum, how often should an emergency action plan be practiced?

      a. Every new season (i.e. fall, winter, spring)
      b. Every two years
      c. Annually
      d. Only when there are changes

98) At minimum, how often should an emergency action plan be practiced?

   a. Every new season (i.e. fall, winter, spring)
   b. Every two years
   c. Annually
      a. All emergency plans should be reviewed and rehearsed annually at minimum. The results of the review should be thoroughly documented. Additionally, this should accompanied with written documentation of any modifications to the emergency action plan.
   d. Only when there are changes

Anderson JC, Courson RW, Kleiner DM, McLoda TA. National Athletic Trainers' Association position statement: Emergency planning in athletics. *J Athl Train*. 2002;37(1):99-104

99) When should the pre-participation examination be completed?

       a. At least 1-2 week before start of preseason
       b. At least 2 weeks before preseason
       c. At least 3 weeks before preseason
       d. At least 4-6 weeks before preseason

99) When should the pre-participation examination be completed?

    a. At least 1-2 week before start of preseason
    b. At least 2 weeks before preseason
    c. At least 3 weeks before preseason
    d. At least 4-6 weeks before preseason
        a. Pre-participation exam should be completed between 4 and 6 weeks prior to preseason to allow for appropriate follow-up for any findings that need further evaluation.

American Academy of Family Physicians, American College of Sports Medicine, American Medical Society for Sports Medicine, American Academy of Pediatrics. *PPE: Preparticipation Physical Evaluation*. 4th ed. Elk Grove Village, IL: American Academy of Pediatrics; 2010.

100) You are the principal investigator of a new research study investigating the number of new cases of rhabdomyolysis in the past year. What is this type of measurement called?

   a. Rate
   b. Incidence
   c. Prevalence
   d. Distribution

100) You are the principal investigator of a new research study investigating the number of new cases of rhabdomyolysis in the past year. What is this type of measurement called?

    a. Rate
    b. Incidence
        a. Incidence is defined as the number of new cases over a specified length of time.
    c. Prevalence
    d. Distribution

Page P. Research designs in sports physical therapy. *Int J Sports Phys Ther*. 2012;7(5):482-482.

Made in the USA
Columbia, SC
25 September 2019